MARTHA GRAHAM

M A R T H A
G R A H A M

*The Evolution of Her Dance Theory
and Training 1926-1991*

Compiled by
MARIAN HOROSKO

a cappella books

Library of Congress Cataloging-in-Publication Data

Martha Graham: the evolution of her dance theory and training/
    compiled by Marian Horosko. — 1st ed.
        p.   cm.
    ISBN 1-55652-142-1: $29.95. — ISBN 1-55652-141-3 (pbk.):
    $14.95
    1. Graham, Martha. 2. Choreographers—United States—
Biography. 3. Dancers—United States—Biography. I. Horosko,
Marian.
GV1785.G7M27   1991
792.8'2'092—dc20
[B]   91-29256
                                                                                CIP

a cappella books
an imprint of
Chicago Review Press, Incorporated
5 4 3 2 1
Printed in the United States of America

Editorial offices:
PO Box 380
Pennington, NJ 08534

Business/sales offices:
814 N. Franklin St.
Chicago, IL 60610

Cover photograph: Martha Graham in *Satyric Festival Song*, choreographed in
1932, photographed in 1940 by Barbara Morgan, courtesy Morgan and Morgan, Dobbs Ferry, NY.

Cover design by Fran Lee
Interior design and editorial direction by Richard Carlin

Interview with Martha Graham reprinted by permission of *Dance Magazine*

921
GRAHAM

Contents

Introduction

In modern dance, one name looms over all others: Martha Graham. Her works influenced the entire growth of dance, not only directly through the dancers that she trained (and, in turn, the many dancers that they trained), but through the impact of her life and work on dance culture. Her revolutionary dance making has been compared to the artistic innovations of Picasso and the musical genius of Stravinsky. Her contribution as a performer, choreographer, and teacher set a standard for a new movement vocabulary. Graham was the most famous, most controversial, and longest-lasting of all of the modern dance pioneers, and her dance school the longest operating school of modern dance in the world.

Martha Graham: The Evolution of Her Dance Theory and Training 1926–1991 is the first book to explore how Graham's unique dance movement developed. Because so many modern dancers study Graham Technique™ today, it is tempting to believe that her dance theory sprang,

1

phoenix-like, from the very first steps she took as a solo artist in 1926. In fact, the Graham training method evolved from sixty-five years of working with dancers and actors, as well as through her life-long work of making new dances.

Despite the lasting legacy of Graham's teaching, there has yet to be a comprehensive evaluation of how her training methods developed throughout her dance career. Graham herself kept the focus away from her contributions to dance training. She somewhat disingenuously made no claim to creating a new technique of movement. "No school of movements," she insisted should be added to her accomplishments; "I have simply rediscovered what the body can do." Of course, it is one thing to discover "what the body can do" and another thing completely to create an entire range of human movements, to train dancers to move more expressively. The dancers who speak in this book testify to Graham's remarkable capabilities as a teacher, whose system of dance training inspired their later careers as dancers, teachers, and choreographers.

Modern dance began as a clear and distinct alternative to ballet. While ballet sought to free the dancer from gravity in its expression, modern dance pulled the dancer back to earth to express the psychological turmoil and issues of the era—a time of change and artistic vitality. Ballet training often was based on a strict, unchanging "syllabus" of movements. Modern dance rejected the strict syllabus, saying that movement should arise naturally from the dancers themselves. While ballet imposed movement on the body, modern dance sought to draw out what was already there, to "simply rediscover what the body can do."

Yet the testimony of the dancers who worked with Graham belies the assertion that she worked without any underlying method. In fact, Graham pioneered many of the teaching methods that are now standard in modern dance pedagogy: floor exercises to strengthen the back and legs; standing balances; the stretch series on the floor with four different arm patterns and levels; open Fourth Position; falls; side extensions; and walks, runs, skips, and leaps across the floor in diagonal were all taught in classes as early as 1927–28.

The famous "contraction and release" principle appeared in Graham's teaching also in the late 1920s. This ancient awareness of the physicality of movement dependent upon the breath and the anatomical changes in the body due to the breathing process was based on her early training in Eastern dance forms in the Denishawn Company. Although Yoga-like breathing was introduced into the classrooms of Western dance at the turn of the century, Graham was the first to develop the contraction and release principle into an inherent principle of movement in her new dance form.

Graham's vocabulary and training evolved through the growth of her choreography. And because new generations of dancers brought different abilities and challenges to her company, her choreography developed in new directions, which was, in turn, mirrored in the technique and training. For instance, in the thirties when the company was composed entirely of women, the dances reflected the social climate of the day with an emphasis on angular, vigorous, and purposeful statements of protest that challenged the concept of "feminine" movement. As new dances were created with new movements, such as the flying leaps in *Celebration*, the training was enlarged and modified to prepare the dancers for performance. In some cases, sections of choreography were lifted intact into the classwork; in other cases, class improvisation found its way into performance.

The 1940s brought a new element to the Graham company: male dancers, most notably Erick Hawkins, a talented dancer who had ballet training. Graham asked Hawkins to teach rudimentary ballet movements to her dancers, as a way of expanding their movement vocabulary. Always a revolutionary, the once fiercely anti-balletic dancer incorporated flexibility, turnout, and lifts into her training and transformed these into an expansion of her own expressivity.

In the fifties and sixties, Graham turned her attention to larger mythic works. She had worked with directors and teachers and taught movement classes to actors at the Neighborhood Playhouse since the late twenties; she now drew on these techniques to give her dancers the training necessary to create her forceful and passionate dramatic creations. As her dancers became more proficient actors, she was able to develop more complex relationships in her works.

In the final phase of her career in the seventies and eighties, Graham created an eclectic style, once more reflecting the changes in her dancers and their expanded movement vocabulary. The dancers now almost universally have a wide range of dance experience and training. And although the distinctions among modern, ballet, jazz, and other dance forms have become blurred, the Graham training regimen remains special in preparing the body—the instrument of dance—for the performance of contemporary dance, because it is organic to the human body, safe, and accumulative in mastery.

In order to study the evolution of Graham's dance teaching, I have combined interviews with dancers who worked with Graham over the last sixty-five years, specifically focusing on Graham's training regimen, along with a complete syllabus of Graham movements. The dancers present a snapshot of the training as it existed during their tenure with the company. Today's syllabus represents the vast accumulation of movements in their basic and varied forms. Together, they give as full a picture as possible of Graham's unique teaching style, a dynamic, growing body of work.

The syllabus is more than just a list of exercises. It includes the teaching cues that Graham used over the years as images for the execution of the movements. Rather than trying to tell a dancer *how* to perform a specific movement, Graham sought to inspire the dancer to do the movement

creatively. Her cues are poetic, impressionistic, and sometimes amusing. She viewed classwork, not as uninspired
repetition, but as a creative process, adjusted to the
individual dancer, but always suited to the standards of
performance. The syllabus is not to be blindly followed,
but to serve as a guide for those who have been trained
in her principles and methodology.

By reading the memories of the dancers who worked
with Graham, we are able to enter the teacher's mind. Not
only can we compare the dance syllabus of the thirties (as
it is remembered by Gertrude Shurr and Sophie Maslow)
to today's method, but we can see how the syllabus fit the
needs of the thirties, just as today's syllabus is suited to
Graham's entire choreographic repertoire. In this way, Graham hewed to the modernist aesthetic to "make it new";
to re-interpret the past for the present. Always the teacher,
Graham liked to describe her training methods by
paraphrasing the words of the philosopher Heraclitus: "The
only [perpetual] constant is change." I hope that this book
will contribute to the continuance of the creative exploration that is the heart of Graham dance training.

ACKNOWLEDGMENTS

In order to understand the development of Graham's dance
theory and training, I decided to assemble a group of dancers
who worked with her through the years. Beate Gordon, of the
Asia Society, consented with enthusiasm to the public use of
the society's Lila Acheson Wallace Auditorium for a day-long
seminar. Madeleine Nichols, curator of the Dance Collection at
the New York Public Library at Lincoln Center, offered her
assistance with the videotaping and sound recording of the
proceedings. After I raised the seed money and set the public-
ity in motion, the date was set for Thursday, May 19, 1988. With
the cooperation of Ron Protas and Linda Hodes, assistant artistic directors of the Martha Graham Dance Company, and Diane

Gray, director of the Martha Graham School of Contemporary Dance, the meeting began to take shape.

Although some former dancers were on tour or out of the country on that date, a representative number who danced from 1926—the date of Graham's first independent concert—to the present were able to participate. Following the seminar, I interviewed several dancers who were unable to attend.

I would like to extend my appreciation to all of the participants in the seminar as well as to those who added their comments afterwards: Erick Hawkins, Bessie Schönberg, John Butler, Bertram Ross, and Christine Dakin. Appreciation also goes to Richard Carlin, of a cappella books, who recognized the value of documenting Graham's training methods, and for publishing this material.

Marian Horosko

Interview with Martha Graham

Interview with Martha Graham on the occasion of her ninety-fifth birthday, May 11, 1989. She observed the birthday year as she had lived: rehearsing, traveling, and making new dances for her Martha Graham Dance Company; overseeing performances by the Martha Graham Ensemble; and watching classes at the Martha Graham School of Contemporary Dance.

Martha Graham lived a short distance from her school. Her apartment was full of small figures and statuettes—symbols of dances she had performed. The apartment was light and immaculate. White orchids in clay pots swayed before billowing, transparent curtains. Spotlights dramatized a coromandel screen. It was a theatrical atmosphere. Graham sat on a white sofa. Her face was softly made up, her dark hair drawn back by a black chiffon scarf worn to frame her small face. Her prominent cheekbones and chiseled profile have identified her on posters and programs for almost a century. She wore a purple satin long-sleeved top with matching trousers. A fur rug covered her slender legs and warmed her hands. She wore a beautiful turquoise American Indian wedding necklace. She pointed it out and wanted you to notice it. She dressed elegantly for this interview because she was going to talk about dance, and because she was a performer.

Q. How do you cast a role?

"When I cast a role," Graham pointed out in her soft-spoken manner, "I look for avidity, an eagerness for life, a blood memory in the sense that the dancer remembers and can call upon more of his or her life than has yet been lived. There has to be a lot of hunger and a need in the dancer. Of course, formal training must be there, but there also has to be courage, a willingness to explore unknown feelings and daring to feel them and let them become a part of your being. It's scary. Terrifying. But you do it because you have no choice.

    "The composer Edgard Varèse once told me that he believed that everyone had genius. But some people have it only for a few minutes. I don't use the word 'genius,' but I think what he meant was that we all have the capacity to live up to our ultimate selves, but most of us don't, or won't. I look for the dancer who will."

Q. Have you ever been disappointed in your choice of a dancer for a role?

"Oh, yes. Sometimes a dancer I have selected is not brave enough to meet the challenge." Roles in Graham works require the emotional challenge of experiencing extremes—

madness to sanity, roughness to tenderness, lust to love, ecstasy to contrition, sin to rejoicing, spirituality to intense sensuality. "There is no training for this. The dancer has to be able to respond to the imagery that shapes a movement, to the logic of why a move is from here to there, and must understand the underlying motives and feelings of a character at a given moment."

Q. You often recite a phrase of a poem, refer to literature, philosophy, a biblical passage, or recount an anecdote. Do today's dancers respond to this kind of imagery?

"Some do, some don't. It has always been so. Some respond to a quote or a saying on a deeper level and are stimulated to search within themselves. Some listen but do not hear. Some look but do not see. Some understand a character but never become that character."

A yardstick used to determine a dancer's success in becoming a character, as well as the yardstick Graham used for her own choice of movement, is her oft-told story about her father catching her, when she was very young, in the telling of a lie. Her father, an alienist—as doctors whose patients had nervous or mental disorders were once called (they would be considered psychiatrists today)—told her that the way he knew she was lying was because of the way she moved. He had learned from his patients that if the words and movements were inconsistent, the patient was lying. Graham never forgot the lesson. "Movement doesn't lie," she repeated emphatically, applying the rule to almost everything. "Either a performance is honest, or it is not."

Q. What do you think of the current practice of performing without makeup or costume because these may obscure movement?

"That is an indulgence. As themselves, without costume or makeup, performers can be quite boring. Dance is theater and larger than life. Makeup and costume, correctly chosen, define movement in a different way."

Graham frequently created her own costumes. Halston, who was her designer from 1975 until his death in 1989, claimed that he was her hands. Costume, for her, has always been used as a metaphor.

Q. Joseph Campbell, in his book *The Power of Myth*, emphasized the importance of myths, tales, and stories in shaping humankind's morality, ethics, and behavior. Was your use of mythological stories for your dances to instruct?

"Not at all. My parents read mythology to me and I remember how it filled me with wonder and fright. The tales fed my imagination. I knew Campbell, of course. He was married to one of my girls [Jean Erdman]. Take the tale of Achilles' heel, for instance. I wanted to know why his heel was left to become his only vulnerable place. Things like that fascinated me, so I made dances about them.

"There are three things I won't talk about," Graham offered: "Politics, religion, and sex. I'm interested in human rights, not politics. That's why I did not accept an invitation from Joseph Goebbels [Hitler's propaganda chief] to appear in Germany in 1936, and why I would not permit my group to perform in South Africa today, if we were asked. As for religion, it's a personal choice. My thoughts are not confined to any one belief system. As for sex, it is holy and sacred. I don't discuss it. For these reasons, I have cast and trained dancers from all parts of the world, from all religions, and both sexes equally. It was never a matter of politics, religion, or sex in my doing so."

Q. What were the influences in your life that helped you formulate your strong opinions?

"There were many mentors and influences, but there was one in particular. I was dancing the lead in *Xochitl* (1920) for the Denishawn Company. One day, a man backstage took me aside and said 'You're a good dancer, and you're intelligent. But you have *something*. I can't describe it, but it's *something*.' He was Alexander Pantages, owner of a chain of theaters that featured vaudeville shows like the one we were appearing in before the movie showing. I was young and impressionable, and I never forgot what he said. I believed it and followed that 'something' ever since. When a wealthy woman offered to send me to study with Mary Wigman in Germany, I refused. I wanted to follow my own 'something.' "

Q. Where is that "something" leading you now?

"I still make dances. I don't call myself a choreographer because that's a big, wonderful word that can cover up a lot of sins. I work. That's what I call what I do when I make dances.

"Dance has changed, and I have changed. We live in a different time, but that is no reason for not reconstructing the dances of the past and performing them now. The past is not dead; it is not even past. People live on inner time; the moment in which a decisive thought or feeling takes place can be at any time. Timeless feelings are common to all of us. A work is dated if it doesn't speak to us about those timeless feelings. It doesn't matter when the work was done, or when those feelings were experienced. The past can be as fresh as now."

Q. What are you working on now? Will you talk about it?

"No. I'm reminded of all the times Miss Ruth [St. Denis] had an idea for a dance, made the costumes, posed for photographs, and then never did the dance. I save all the energy for rehearsing, and I don't want to dissipate those ideas by talking about them. I use my energy for that. The energy of the world is available to all of us. It moves the planets and makes everything work. We can all use it. Only we become frightened or frustrated or too tired to use it. I use it."

Q. In 1987, Rudolf Nureyev and Mikhail Baryshnikov danced *Appalachian Spring* at the opening of the Graham season. Later in the same season, Baryshnikov danced *El Penitente.* How did you teach these two ballet stars their roles?

"They saw videocassettes and had an idea about the work, but first learned the phrases, then accommodated their bodies. I did that with them, but I don't know how we did it. They were absolutely responsive to trying new movements and excited about it. It was new for them and new for me. It's hard to know how people learn. Some learn visually through videocassettes, some learn physically. But both artists were free of preconceived notions and open to every suggestion."

Q. Are there any other choreographers who might be invited to work with your company?

"There is always the possibility that someone from our company may emerge, as did Merce Cunningham, Yuriko, and Paul Taylor, with a work we can perform. We are always looking for possibilities. Form and structure cannot be taught but will emerge from what has to be said. But first of all, the technique must be mastered and understood to perfection. Let me give an example. In reconstructing *Celebration* this year, no one could remember the ending. Sophie Maslow, Yuriko, Linda Hodes, and Ron Protas all created suitable closing moments for me to see and redo. I chose the one Ron worked out without knowing he did it. My point is that I have two associate artistic directors, Ron Protas and Linda Hodes, in whom I have confidence to know what I want, whom I have trained, and who have produced suitable artistic standards for my dances for a number of years.

"Often it is said that I, at my age, cannot possibly attend to all aspects of my company and school. This is true to a point. The rehearsing and coaching duties have fallen to my two associate directors, and the teaching to those who were company members and have remained with me. But I still make my own dances, oversee the lighting, the costumes, and coach the final rehearsals.

"I'd like to clear up two points that have troubled me over the years. It disturbs me deeply that some dancers date my technique from the time they learned it and know only one aspect of it. They limit themselves and their own knowledge by not having an overview from the time they studied to the present.

"The other point concerns claims that I have or have had codirectors. A long time ago, I decided that my place was front and center. That's where I chose to be, and that's where I remain."

PART ONE

Witnesses to the Technique

I

The First Years

Martha Graham was born in Allegheny, Pennsylvania in 1894, the daughter of a physician. In 1908, the family resettled in Santa Barbara, California, and Graham began her dance training in the famous Denishawn School in 1916.

Ruth St. Denis (1879-1968) and Ted Shawn (1891-1972) were tireless promoters of modern dance, and their company, Denishawn, became the first truly popular touring ensemble. Their dance style was an amalgam of pseudo-Oriental, American Indian, Far Eastern, and other "exotic" styles that were popular on the vaudeville circuit. Along with these exotic styles, they also experimented with what St. Denis called color and music visualizations, early abstract dances that pointed the way for the modern dance that followed. As teachers, they were highly influential, and from their company the three key originators of modern dance came: Martha Graham, Doris Humphrey, and Charles Weidman. Graham was a favorite of Shawn's, who choreographed solos for her that caught the eye of theatrical promoters in New York.

In the mid-twenties, Graham was invited to perform as a soloist in the popular *Greenwich Village Follies*, her first break with the Denishawn Company. She was also asked to teach at the Eastman School of Music in Rochester, New York. Shawn and St. Denis jealously guarded the Denishawn curriculum, requiring even favored excompany members such as Graham to pay a fee if they wished to teach their dance movement. This proved to be a blessing in disguise, because it forced Graham (and Humphrey and Weidman when they left the Denishawn fold in 1927) to evolve her own teaching methods.

Although her first solos showed the strong Orientalism of Denishawn, Graham was soon moving into the percussive movement that would be a hallmark of her style in the thirties. In the following memories of some of her first students and members of her first dance company, we see how her movement principles were developed through her dance classes.

EVELYN SABIN MANNES

Evelyn Sabin Mannes danced in Graham's first recital in 1926, and remained in the group until 1930.

I was a pupil of Martha Graham in 1925 when she came to teach at the Eastman School of Music in Rochester. When she chose not to return for a second year, I came to New York—at the age of eighteen—to continue to study with her and was a member of her first small group, The Trio. After some years, I had to leave New York because of illness. Eventually, I danced and taught in Rochester until my marriage in 1940.

When Martha Graham came to teach in Rochester, I think she was already committed to creating her own dance, uniquely her own. In retrospect, I think our dances in those days may have been, quite naturally, somewhat reminiscent of Denishawn, where she had her own training and was a leading member of the company. No such thought ever occurred to me at the time. I had never seen any Denishawn dancing and had studied ballet before coming to Martha.

The movement, to me, was always changing, developing, and growing. And I think now that in the most elementary, and perhaps fundamental way, we took first steps toward the great future that has evolved so phenomenally.

I know that through the years the technique and its teaching have become more formalized. I don't even know its vocabulary so I shall have to refer to it as simply as we did sixty years ago: walking, running, jumping, leaping, contraction and release, the floorwork, and the falls. These are the movements that I recognize, remember, and feel as I see the company in performance. I have never watched a class.

In the beginning, we were taught only by Martha. For the concerts, there was no orchestra. Louis Horst was always at the piano. Everything we did, in so far as we were able, was done in Martha's way. The inspiration and the vision were always there.

AILES GILMOUR

Ailes Gilmour is the sister of the late sculptor, Isamu Noguchi. She was a member of the Graham company from 1929–1933. She began her study of dance at the Neighborhood Playhouse in New York City and performed with the Graham Company at the opening of the Radio City Music Hall. In 1929, she introduced her brother Isamu to the "young, new dancer and her approach to movement." She worked with the New Dance League, the Workers' Dance League, and shared recitals with Bill Matons' Experimental Unit in the 1930s.

I was born in Yokohama, Japan. My mother was the Scotch-Irish writer Leonie Gilmour—whose name I use; my father was a Japanese poet. I came to San Francisco in 1920, and moved East to attend the Ethical Culture School; their educational philosophy influenced my mother. I was graduated from a boarding school in Connecticut in 1929, and then applied to the Neighborhood Playhouse in New York City for a "living scholarship"—a fifteen-dollar-a-week stipend for food, lodging, and free tuition.

At that time, fifteen dollars was sufficient living money and enabled the students at the Playhouse to study the arts of speech, drama, and dance. It was there that I studied under the direction of a brilliant and blazing new dancer—Martha Graham. I had seen her dance in *Adolescence* (1929) and was now afforded the opportunity to study with her and learned her new concepts of movement based upon contraction and release. The same year, 1929, she asked me to join her professional group; that year she choreographed *Heretic*, to music based upon old Breton songs.

The public was not used to the starkness and simplicity of movement in her work. It was not "pretty" and contained none of the conventions of ballet. It was a complete break from tradition. People unused to the bare bones of dance were often repelled. I loved it! There, it seemed, was truth.

We made our own costumes. Even the leotards used in class were cut from a yard of old jersey split like a diamond where we sewed the crotch. We wore these in class and danced to music played on the piano by Enid Dareman. Louis Horst, Martha's musical mentor who wrote much of her music, also gave classes at the Playhouse. We studied all of the arts related to theater: movement, voice, music, and stage sets. It was a new and exciting world.

When Martha won a Guggenheim Fellowship, she went to Mexico and was influenced by that country's religious fervor. She created *Primitive Mysteries* (1931). Again, we sewed our own costumes, tubular wool jerseys fashioned so tightly to our bodies that there was little room to move. Wearing it was to become a piece of sculpture as our bodies strained against the tubing. Martha was the Virgin in white organdy, like a flower blooming above the dark mass. It was simple, direct, and powerful.

My brother, Isamu Noguchi, designed the set for *Dark Meadow* in 1946 with music by Carlos Chavez. I introduced Isamu to Graham in 1929 when he was attracting the interest of people in the art world. He was interested in "the young dancer with a new concept of movement" and worked out several sets for her. Eventually, over the years, Noguchi would create sets for more than twenty works including: *Frontier* (1935, from *Perspectives*), *Chronicle* (1936), *Appalachian Spring* (1944), *Cave of the Heart* (1946), *Errand into the Maze* (1947), *Night Journey* (1947), *Clytemnestra* (1958), and *Embattled Garden* (1958).

On December 27, 1932, Radio City Music Hall opened as a place for concert artists. In addition to the Graham company, dancers Harald Kreutzberg and his partner Yvonne Georgi, and Ray Bolger (the tap dancer) were on the program. The conductor was Leopold Stokowski. When we danced on the enormous stage, *The New Yorker* magazine described us as looking like mice racing across the vast expanse.

At the end of our debut in *Choric Pattern*, "Roxy" (Samuel L. Rothafel), the founder of Radio City Music Hall, would sit in the center of the auditorium where he could play out all manner of visual effects. He was keen to have us appear through a steam curtain, but Martha explained that our costumes were all wool and that the steam would shrink the material and immobilize us!

We had a short run, a week as I recall. Radio City was not a success until it became a movie house with the Rockettes.

I took classes with Martha at the Neighborhood Playhouse by day and again at her studio at night. We would rehearse until one or two in the morning and Martha would give us rye bread and cheese to eat at the end of rehearsal. We never got paid. It was a wonderful time to live and work. I will always remember Martha, and I'm honored to have worked with her.

BESSIE SCHÖNBERG

Bessie Schönberg was a member of the Martha Graham Dance Company from 1930–1931, a career cut short by an injury. As an educator, however, she holds an eminent position in teaching composition and in 1987 was awarded the New York Dance and Performance citation (aka the "Bessie") for her lifetime achievement.

Schönberg studied Dalcroze Eurythmics in Dresden, Germany, attended the University of Oregon, and received a BA from Bennington College. In New York City, she studied with Graham at the Neighborhood Playhouse and soon joined her company. As a teacher, Schönberg was a member of the performing arts faculty at Sarah Lawrence College from 1938–1975, as well as the director of dance and theater. In addition, she has taught at Briarcliff Junior College, the New Dance Group, the Juilliard School of Music, the Bennington School of Dance, and directed many operas and musical theater productions.

Since her retirement, she has been a guest teacher at the City College of New York, Ohio State University, Wesleyan University, and at London's Contemporary Dance Center. Presently, she is artistic advisor to choreographers at The Yard at Chilmark on Martha's Vineyard.

Schönberg has served on the dance panel of the New York State Council on the Arts, the advisory panel of the National Endowment for the Arts, and is chairman of the board of directors of Dance Theater Workshop.

It was a fast, amazing, heady time for me, unexpected and undeserved as well, to be taken into the Graham company.

I grew up in Dresden where my father was responsible for my seeing everything that was going on in the name of dance. I saw Wigman in all her early years there, and Kreutzberg, and the Wiesenthals. But dancing was completely out.

I was allowed to take some Dalcroze, not in the original institute where Jacques Dalcroze started, but in the city, in a little vegetarian restaurant where the classes were held in the dining room.

I came to America in 1926 because my mother was a voice and opera workshop teacher at the University of Oregon in Eugene. I became a painting and sculpture student there and took dance from a disciple of Margaret H'Doubler, because we all had to have some physical education. It was hard to take for someone who had been brought up on Wigman. Fortunately, Martha Hill took the job when the other teacher retired and the classes became one of the great experiences of my life. Hill had been in New York earlier and taken a summer course with Graham. She came to Eugene in 1927; by 1929, we both left and headed for New York and the Neighborhood Playhouse.

I watched Graham's class and was breathless, speechless, and tongue-tied at meeting her. Hill introduced me and I was overcome. She suggested that we, and a fellow teacher from Oregon who was with us (Mary Jo Shelley), go to the apartment of Mrs. Rita Morgenthau, the executive director of the school, in the hope that we might be given scholarships. I got a scholarship and fifteen dollars per week.

My first class was at Ruth Doing's second floor studio, around the corner from Carnegie Hall on 56th Street (Martha's studio was on West 10th Street at that time). After my first class, Martha asked me to come into the company. It was all too quick.

The first class that I watched was very physical. Martha seemed to be able to do anything she wanted with her body. She had the schooling, but she also had a God-given strength and flexibility. She had little square feet that were elastic as well as strong, and she was small with long, black hair and had an incredible extension.

As I remember the classes at that time, we did stretches on the floor, some standing exercises, and a lot of moving in circles. I remember an amusing thing: before the class, Louis Horst would play Percy Grainger's *Country Gardens* and we would move around in a circle in a run to warmup. I loved it, cutting through the studio as fast as I could go. It was wonderful. It's still a good warmup. Then we began the formal class.

Later in the classes, we did triplets with a change of accent and change of direction. Twisting on the floor and spirals were important. I remember once saying, shyly, to Martha that the exercises reminded me of a snake dancing on its tail and she responded that that was exactly the image I should have. She meant that there should be no weight on the floor and the body should be almost supported in suspension. As I remember, in the 1930s, the contraction was executed as a lifting up, and the release, as a pressing down. I don't believe they do that any more. All the percussive exercises we used to do are not done any longer. Time and Martha moved on into a more romantic and lyrical, even voluptuous, quality of movement.

Classes at the Neighborhood Playhouse were all day—voice, acting, Horst's composition classes, other things, and, of course, Martha's technique classes.

As a new student, I would go back to my little room in the International House, where I was staying, and spend half the night trying to learn what I was supposed to have learned in the class. I worked at it. Then, the next day, I would find Martha saying, "Forget what we learned yesterday, it's all changed now." This was part of the freshness of being involved with her; the changes and paths she took were no mystery. She knew where she was going.

As I look back, there was a continual transition for Martha from the Delsarte and Denishawn training into her own path. A deep influence, not frequently mentioned, on her path was the Japanese dancer, Michio Ito. She was with him in the *Greenwich Village Follies* and then in *Nuages*, the first time it was performed in a Lewisohn production. (The Lewisohn Stadium performances in Manhattan were presented free of charge in the outdoor theater during the summer months. Major companies and performers were presented.)

I remember dancing in at least two of Irene Lewisohn's "Orchestral Dramas." The stars were Martha Graham, Charles Weidman, Blanche Talmud, and others, as well as scholarship students from the Playhouse like myself (Anna Sokolow, Sophie Maslow, Ailes Gilmour, and others). Nikolai Sokoloff and the Cleveland Symphony were engaged for the productions. These were performed, one at the YMHA at 92nd Street and Lexing-

ton Avenue; the other at City Center Theatre on 55th Street called
the "Mecca Temple" at that time, but were not performed at
the Lewisohn Stadium.

Ruth St. Denis influenced Martha to some extent. She taught
in a free-wheeling manner, totally concentrated on the subject
one minute, then deciding to change using the words: "That's
boring. Let's do something else." But she was fabulous, partially exotic, and partially practical. And, of course, as everyone
knows, she was very beautiful and good natured. I tell you this
because I think she was a visual influence on Graham, although
I feel that Ted Shawn was a greater influence on her early training. Shawn gave her many opportunities and she was a soloist
in his choreography for the Denishawn Company. Although he
was not as theatrical as Ruth, he was more methodical. Graham,
of course, rejected a lot, as well.

I was placed immediately in the company and was quite
favored. I think it was my passionate desire to dance and my
eagerness that did it for me. My first dances were *Moment Rustica*
(1929) which had a peasant quality, and *Danse Languide* (1926),
a leftover from Graham's first concert. It was danced by Evelyn
Sabin (Mannes), Betty Macdonald, and Rosina Savelli, who
replaced Thelma Biracree that first summer in 1926. *Languide* had
a very sculptural quality because of its long, long scarves and
full backbends on the knees. I was thrilled. Betty and Rosina were
still in the company at that time, but Evelyn had left. They would
come back from time to time, if they were needed, for a tour.

By the thirties, we were living in a period of primitive art.
It was emulated everywhere, and Martha was part of that movement in dance. Her movements were simple, strong, straight,
and percussive. Those were the terms in which she was creating her dances. She packed movement into the instant of action.
It was frustrating and exciting at the same time: a boiling point
that was never really reached.

Unlike Wigman, who believed in an extraordinary, almost
Oriental way of turning out the leg, Graham surprised me with
her Barlach-like starkness during that period.* Her changes in
her movements made them purer, or starker, as I saw it. More

---

* Ernst Barlach (1870–1938) was a German sculptor, graphic artist, and playwright,
whose powerful figures in bronze or wood owe much to a very personal combination
of Gothic and cubist influences.

and more was stripped way. I remember seeing her in *Dance* (1929) on a little platform in a red dress, moving between the shoulders and the knees. That was it. It was powerful.

In class, we did *calls,* a twist in the torso in a percussive movement that pulled one arm up as if to call someone to follow. They are circular movements, in part. The audience was supposed to finish the circle for themselves.

Primitive Mysteries (1931) and *Heretic* (1929) were my greatest experiences with Graham. In *Primitive Mysteries*, Louis Horst counted on me to set the tempo for him in each of the three sections that had a silent introduction and a silent exodus. So I was the first to come out on stage. It was with a very sharp walk that we began. Performances now don't seem to have that same bite. We worked on nothing but that bite in the movement.

Heretic was created by Graham in one night. I've never seen anyone before or since work that way, and I've seen a great deal of dance. Louis had found a very beautiful Breton song that had a verse and a chorus. It was percussive in quality, and searing, as Martha put herself against a wall of resistance—the chorus of dancers. Of course, it could be interpreted as Martha, herself, against tradition or whatever you want to interpret there. It was a pleading figure against a hostile group—terse, brief, stark; I think no other dance quite represented her personal statement with such power, although all her dances were personal statements.

At this time, these were dances of the people. Although she was not of the people, her sympathies at that time were with the downtrodden.

The positions we held were you might call struck, sustained, with changes made on three counts. They were big changes made in the whole group. We sometimes stepped on one another, but you had to keep the meaning with tremendous concentration. Graham had almost eliminated movement of the arms, and they were thrown straight up or held down. The group was almost wooden, but she was alive, and very lyrical by contrast.

I was in some of the Lewisohn performances, and those at Bennington College, but my career was cut short by a knee injury, a torn cartilage. We didn't trust operations in those days. Martha was gentle and understanding when I went to class but this was a total accident that I had had. I wasn't warmed up enough, I think. In those days, we were young and thought ourselves invincible. We have since had to learn how to prepare the body for classes and performances. But I could no longer dance. It was over.

As I look back, dance seemed simpler and deeper. There were just a few people working at that time and each—Doris Humphrey, Hanya Holm, Charles Weidman, Helen Tamiris, and Martha Graham—were almost monastic within themselves. They were so dedicated and single-visioned in dance as they thought it should be. All these people seemed not quite of this earth, although Martha I knew was very much of this earth—gossiping with us as we sewed our costumes, then far, far ahead of us when she brought back her thoughts to us in the studio.

Graham dances look different to me today because the dancing technique has changed; it has been developed, opened, and widened in every aspect. Compared to the group in the thirties, the current company dances differently. Although the dancing has a totally different look, it is extraordinarily beautiful.

My memories are of my own excitement and deep commitment in a euphoric beginning.

II

The Thirties

T he thirties was a key decade in the development of Graham's work as a teacher and a choreographer. It was during this decade that her all-female dance company reached its maturity, and many legendary dancers—such as Sophie Maslow, May O'Donnell, and Anna Sokolow—performed with her. Some of her most famous dances were premiered by this ensemble, including *Primitive Mysteries* (1931), *Celebration* (1934), and *Deep Song* (1937).

A key player in Graham's growth as a teacher and a choreographer was pianist/composer Louis Horst (1884-1964). Horst was an accompanist at the Denishawn School who befriended all of the modern dancers. He developed an especially close relationship with Graham, often teaching class for her when she was unavailable, and developing a system of teaching modern dance choreography that influenced an entire generation of dancers. He scored many of Graham's dances of the thirties and also founded the influential journal, *Dance Observer*, in 1934, a paper with a definite pro-Graham slant.

The dancers of the thirties who worked with Graham comment on the growth of a more formal dance class. Gertrude Shurr gives a detailed ''syllabus'' for a typical class of the era, while Sophie Maslow gives a more impressionistic description of classwork. It is clear that, as Graham matured as a creative artist, she needed to develop a methodology for training her dancers to achieve her special vision. The dance class became this training ground. But, equally important, the class became an experimental laboratory where training could serve as a catalyst for further creativity.

GERTRUDE SHURR

Gertrude Shurr began her career at the Denishawn School and danced solo performances of the early Denishawn dances (1925–1929), which were interpolated into musical acts developed for production of the movie prologues of that day. She danced in the first Humphrey-Weidman concerts (1927–1929) and, at the same time, began to study with Martha Graham.

Shurr became a Graham teacher and a member of the Martha Graham Dance Company from 1930–1938. Her other professional experiences include more than forty years with the Shurr-O'Donnell Studio of Modern Dance in New York City. (May O'Donnell, as well, was a member of the Graham company from 1932–1938 and 1943–1953.)

Shurr established with O'Donnell the San Francisco Dance Theater. Later, she became a teacher and chairman of the dance department of New York's High School for the Performing Arts, 1957–1973, for which she earned commendation in 1973.

She is a lifetime member of the Arizona Dance Arts Alliance and is currently working on her book, The Roots of American Modern Dance, *from which the following is an excerpt. She currently lives in Tucson, Arizona.*

The first time I saw Martha Graham was during the 1926 summer session of the Denishawn School. This was a Sunday morning in Studio 61 in Carnegie Hall, just a week or two before the Denishawn Company left for their tour of the Orient. I was at the studio to see a performance of the Swedish dancer, Ronnie

Johansson*, the first European modern dancer we had ever seen. This particular performance was an audition for Ronnie Johansson, for the possibility of including her dances as an added attraction in the Denishawn programs. It did not work out that way. Her *Pierrot* and *Waltzes* did not fit into the programs.

The entire Denishawn Company was there, and since I was a scholarship student and worked in the office, I was permitted to be present. Louis Horst brought Martha Graham to this performance. Everyone knew Martha. She was a great dancer who had left the Denishawn Company to dance in the *Greenwich Village Follies*. Miss Ruth [St. Denis] had no plans for Martha to join the forthcoming tour of the Orient. Martha was short, had long black hair, a long face with enormous eyes, and was very, very thin. She really looked what was thought to be Oriental. Miss Ruth was not about to take "coals to Newcastle." In fact, Miss Ruth preferred the long-stemmed American beauty type of dancer, the clean-cut American look, mostly blonde and fair. Martha was just the opposite. Martha wanted to go to the Orient, but it was not to be with Denishawn. Years later, Graham took her own company to the Orient to great acclaim.

The next time I saw Martha Graham was at her concert performances in 1926 and 1927. All I can remember was how beautiful the concerts were. I cried. I wanted to dance like Martha; the exquisite Oriental touches that were inbred in her from Denishawn; the lyrical qualities in the Debussy series; the subtle touches of comedy in her satires. It was all quite wonderful. Did I see the future Martha Graham at that time? I do not know. All I knew was that I wanted to study with her and dance in her company.

It wasn't until 1928 that Martha's dramatic approach to dance was evident. More angular physical movement and sharper dynamics appeared in her *Revolt*, *Immigrant Series*, and *Poems of 1917*, showing another side of Martha—her dramatic urge to communicate, her subtle comedy, her strong satire, and her exqui-

---

* Ronnie Johansson was a Swedish dancer and teacher, born in Riga, Latvia, in 1891. She went to Stockholm in 1913; studied modern dance there and in Germany; toured Europe (1918–1925); came to the US where she was assistant teacher at the Denishawn School; and gave a series of recitals and demonstrations in colleges and universities. She opened her own school in Stockholm (1932) and became a teacher at the Royal Dramatic Theater (1942).

site use of materials as in *Tanagra*. Now, more than ever, I wanted to study with Graham.

I knew Martha had left the *Greenwich Village Follies* and was teaching in Rochester, New York, at the Eastman School of Music three days a week and three days a week at the John Murray Anderson School of Theater on East 58th Street in New York City. I also knew she was preparing for a New York concert with three of her Rochester students. I really wanted to go to Rochester and study with Martha Graham.

At this time, a friend of mine who danced in the movie prologue productions that John Murray Anderson produced and sent out on the road told me Martha Graham was teaching a children's class one afternoon a week at the school. I knew John Murray Anderson, and I asked him if I could join the class. He told me to speak to his brother Hubert who was in charge of the school. Hubert told me that Martha had a children's class of only three children at that time, but he doubted whether she would take me on as a pupil. I suppose I looked devastated. After an uncomfortable silence for both of us, he said, "Why don't you go and try it?" That was all I needed to hear. The next day, I was in class. I was not much bigger than the three girls, Ruth, Hope, and Rosina, and with my hair in a ponytail, I could easily pass for one of them. I never knew if anyone spoke to Martha about me. She never spoke to me. I just appeared and took the class each week until the end of the year.

The children's class was lovely. Martha gave direction in a sweet, quiet voice, and explained what she wanted and the class followed. Since I missed the beginning of the session, I did not know how Martha introduced her technique. The three girls seemed to know what to do and did it well. We sat on the floor and did a series of exercises to strengthen the back and develop flexibility of the hip. We did leg extensions to straighten the knees and flexion and extension of the feet. I don't recall Martha ever using the terms "contraction" and "release" at this time. The emphasis was placed on strengthening the back and legs. We stood up and did a series of knee bends, which later developed into the first of the lift series. We also performed this exercise with changes of arm patterns. Leg swings and torso and arm swings were performed on different levels. Then the class began with movement across the floor in walks, runs, skips, and leaps on a diagonal or in a circle. At the time, Martha was speaking of the quality of the movement she wanted the class to experience. It seemed a very short hour. I loved it and wanted more.

The next time I saw Martha outside the classroom was at the Denishawn House on West 28th Street. This three-story brownstone house with its twenty-foot ceilings was reconstructed into dance studios with one large studio, a library, and an office on the first floor; a smaller studio and dressing room was on the second floor. The third floor, or attic, was arranged for use as a dormitory for the male scholarship students. The men from the Denishawn Company lived there when they were in town.

When Louis Horst came back from his trip to Vienna, he lived in the Denishawn attic until he found his own apartment. Louis played the piano for most of the classes at the Denishawn School. At this time, I was on a work scholarship at the Denishawn School, which required that I buzz into the evening classes and take attendance. I took the advanced class in the morning. After one of these classes, Louis came out of the classroom and told me he was expecting Martha Graham and would I see that she waited for him in the library. From that moment on, I was a basket case. What should I say? How should I say it? How could I tell Martha what her classes meant to me? I kept practicing many opening sentences. Martha arrived and I said, "Louis said to please wait in the library, he may be a minute or two late." Martha, without saying a word, walked over to the bookcase and stood there reading titles. Finally, class was over and Louis came out. He knew of my experience in Martha's class and how much I wanted to speak with her. He called me over and introduced me with, "Martha, this is a fan of yours!" I was so mad I couldn't say a word. I kept hearing—"a fan of yours," "a fan of yours," over and over again. I could not speak, and my big chance of a great "thank you" speech to Martha Graham was gone. Later on, I discovered that Louis was a baseball fan and often took Martha to baseball games. I realized that being a fan was a special compliment. It was then that I forgave Louis.

While the Denishawn Company was touring the Orient, I was busy teaching the beginning classes at Denishawn, and learning and performing the Denishawn dances. After I left Denishawn, I stayed with Doris Humphrey and Charles Weidman until they gave their first New York concert in 1927. Louis Horst played for their rehearsals and the concert. This gave me a chance to speak to Louis every day, and I finally talked him into letting me form an adult evening class for Martha. The big studio at the John Murray Anderson School was made available to her at night. I started recruiting students for her class. Some were dancers from the Denishawn School, some from the Duncan School, and some were ballet dancers from various ballet studios. I finally recruited a sizeable class.

Martha began to teach in earnest. I knew she could not teach any Denishawn technique because the rule was that no one could use any Denishawn technique or dances without a five hundred dollar payment to the main school. Martha never had that kind of money. In a way, that was a blessing in disguise. She had to develop a movement series of her own so she could teach her students. Martha knew what techniques were needed to train a dancer and that was what she began to do—train dancers. It was in these evening classes that certain teaching phrases began to appear in order to explain or enhance the movement patterns. It was the first time (1927–1928) that Martha used the terms "contraction" and "release" as an awareness of a whole new approach to the physicality of movement dependent upon the breath, and the anatomical changes in the body due to the breathing process.

It was this awareness of the changes of the body due to breathing in and breathing out that freed Martha Graham from her Denishawn ethnic influence as well as the ballet influence. She had found a way to create her own dances, using the contraction and release principle. She found the answer to her own need to discover and explore what the body could do. Martha would often say: "Don't say I invented a school of movement. I only rediscovered what the human body can do." This freed her to explore an infinite variety of movements for her need to communicate through dance.

It was in the evening classes that many "firsts" occurred. The class started on the floor—this was a first. What dance class began before this with the students seated on the floor? After a few stretching exercises for flexibility and leg extensions to the front and side, the dance technique portion of the class began. We sat upright on the hips, knees bent, soles of the feet touching, hands on the ankles, arms rounded, and the torso stretched tall. This was the first sitting position. It was in this position that Martha introduced us to the contraction and release principle.

She concentrated on the body changes that took place as a result of the inhalation and exhalation of breath. Martha wanted to know how the body responded when the breath was exhaled; what happened to the bones; the skeletal part of the body. What happened to the muscles, and what was the quality of movement as a result of this activity. The body changes that took place upon the exhalation of air was called a contraction. The body changes that took place upon the inhalation of air was called a release. This was not a great mystery of life, but a natural phenomenon.

Martha, seated in this first sitting position, demonstrated the movements and made us aware of the body movement inherent in the contraction and release. We soon became aware of the skeletal and muscular movements involved. We found that upon the exhaling of breath, the skeleton or bones of the body moved: the pelvic bone tipped forward, the cartilage of the spine allowed the spine to stretch and curve backward, and the shoulders moved forward, always retaining the alignment of shoulder over hip, while never lowering the level of the seated position. When the breath was inhaled, the skeleton resumed its original position moving to that position in the same order as in the contraction: hip, spine, shoulders. The muscles moved with the skeleton. When the breath is out of the torso, the back muscles stretch and the front muscles shorten. The muscles return to their original position upon the release. This is the anatomical movement of the contraction and release. The anatomical count for this was: hip (1); spine (2); shoulders (3). This count was constant.

Martha developed movement patterns in the first sitting position. These patterns usually started with a simple movement pattern as a theme, that became a long dance pattern with the addition of arm and leg patterns, and changes of direction and levels. For the advanced student, Martha's emphasis was on the technical movement patterns that she was performing at the time. Martha's explanation for these movements was focused primarily on the quality of the movement she wanted. As her assistant, I approached the explanation of the contraction and release from the anatomical point of view for the beginning students.

We also began to sense the quality of movement within the contraction and release. Martha wanted to give us the feeling of the depth of movement. We were not to be two-dimensional.

We had to feel the inner skeleton of the body as part of the whole movement. The deep dramatic quality came on the exhalation of the breath or the contraction; the lyric and open quality on the inhalation of the breath or the release.

When Martha first started teaching, her movements were quite rounded and lyrical. As she began exploring movement for her own dances, she added some of these movement patterns to her technique vocabulary. She also employed "teaching cues": for instance, she would say, "Don't slump on contractions. It's a high, elevated torso in the contraction position." She also added imagery to improve her student's learning progress. She explored what she called the "cut-off-point of sustaining movement," and "of holding a movement, not daring to move, but moving." Other phrases that added imagery were:

> Move on a stationary base.
> Move through space, not as just a hop, skip, and jump.
> Carve a place for yourself in space.
> Project through space as if space were opaque.
> Focus through space, not just up and down.
> The hip is the motivator of movement.
> Contraction is ecstasy as well as despair.
> Free the head, up and back, not down and back.
> Both lyric and dramatic movement must be strong.
> Lengthen the sides of the neck.
> The listening ear, in space and within.
> The hands and feet must respond to the contraction and release.
> There must be a complete articulation of the foot; all the bones of the foot must move.
> The hip bone must move as the jewel in the watch movement.
> There must be an inner depth of movement on the contraction.

These and other phrases were additional firsts in making us aware of the physicality and quality of movement.

Other firsts Martha gave to dance besides the use of the floor, which developed a strong back without the problem of working upright, standing balance, as well as the stretch series on the floor with four different arm patterns and levels—floor, waist, shoulders, and overhead—were the open Fourth Position and its many patterns of movement; the beginning of the series of falls from the seated hip position; the side extensions; movement patterns with changes of levels and changes of direction seated on a stationary base; the use of the hip as the motivating factor for movement; and the challenge of encompassing space on a stationary base. All these forced a deeper use of the exploration of the workings of the human body and the use of the space around it.

Graham technique, as it is now known, came about in several ways. Some of it came from experimentation, some from a simplified version of movements from one of Graham's dances, and some movements were devised to aid a technical need of the class or the dance company. Finally, the technique began to be quite codified and the class quite structured. This, I believe was about 1929–1930. One half hour of the class was spent seated on the floor, one half hour was standing, and one half hour moving across the floor.

Martha's use of a simple theme and variations, changes of levels, arm patterns, and directions made the count of each technique pattern varied. The measures were not always in counts of four or eight. She introduced us to patterns with new counts, sometimes a slow four as a theme of movement, a three count for a lyrical quality, and a percussive or elevation quality on a two count or even an "and-one" count. This change of accent and counts, mixed rhythms, and uneven measures were additional firsts and Martha used them a great deal. Patterns of ten or five counts were not unusual.

Later, three events compelled Martha to further codify and structure her technique and her teaching in class. It was while she was teaching at the Neighborhood Playhouse School of the Theatre* in New York City that she simplified movement patterns and added imagery to help nondancers (actors) understand

---

* The Neighborhood Playhouse School of the Theatre was founded in 1928 by Irene and Alice Lewisohn to further the training developed for their specialized productions, including lyric forms and drama. The first small group of students had the privilege of being taught by Martha Graham, Louis Horst, and Laura Elliot.

and learn more easily this new and exciting activity. It was at the Playhouse that Martha first used the verbal consonant "ess-s-s-s-s. . ." on the contraction or exhalation of the breath, in order to dramatize this physical activity.

The second event was the culminating demonstration at the end of the first summer session at Bennington College in Vermont in 1934. This was a technical demonstration of six weeks of student dance training presented by all the faculty and their Bennington students. Doris Humphrey and Charles Weidman, with their assistants Leticia Ide and José Limón, led their students and demonstrated Humphrey's "fall and recovery" principle, and Weidman's "kinetic movement" patterns. Hanya Holm, with Louise Kloepper as her assistant, led her students and demonstrated her "tension and relaxation" principle. Martha, with me as her assistant, demonstrated her "contraction and release" principle. This was a very special first because it was the first time the public became aware of the differences among these three schools: Humphrey/Weidman, Holm, and Graham.

A definite time limit for the demonstration was given and the technique that had been learned over a short six-week period was demonstrated by beginning students. Martha's demonstration included the following:

I   *Class seated on the floor*

1. Hip warmup and bounces
2. Leg extension, front and sides
3. Foot flexions and extension
4. First seated position
   a. Introduction of contraction and release
   b. Contraction and release with arm and head changes
   c. Change of rhythmic pattern with resulting change in quality of movement
5. Stretches with arm patterns in four levels
6. Open Fourth Position: arm patterns, and hip-motivated direction changes, quarter turn, half turn
7. Back leg extensions with arm pattern
8. Preparation for backfall, seated on both hips, on counts of four, three, two, and a fast one count

9. Seated on both knees: exercise on six—a complete circle of the torso

10. Body upright on both knees: changes of levels with hip swings, leading to the backfall

11. A movement transition to the standing position

II *Standing position and center work in place*

1. Knee bends in First and Second, side-to-side movement, arm patterns, concentric circle patterns with arms

2. Series of lifts, center front, quarter turn, half turn, whole turn on a stationary base, use of arms

3. Brushes: three different levels, front and side

4. Extension patterns of legs: front, side, and on a contraction

5. Hip thrust series

6. Cross-sit in contraction and release and half turns

7. Prancing preparation: prances center and with quarter turn

8. Back roll with change of rhythmic pattern

9. Running in place: change of directions with back roll

10. Jumps in place in First and Second; jump with one knee bent, other leg straight; jump with two knees bent, soles of feet touching; jumps with turns on eight counts; quarter, half, and full turns

11. Side falls from standing position; on a contraction; on counts four, three, and two

12. Backfall on contraction and release

III *Movement across the floor*

1. Walking, running, skipping, leaping: different preparations for leaps and jumps; one- or three-step preparations

2. Leaps across the floor: both knees bent; front knee bent; back leg straight; leg straight in front, bent in back; brush leaps; leaps with both legs straight; split leaps

3. Triplets, with walks, with runs, with leaps

The third event was a lecture demonstration at the New School for Social Research in New York City in 1935 or 1936. It was under the sponsorship of John Martin, and presented the companies of Doris Humphrey, Charles Weidman, Martha Graham, and Hanya Holm demonstrating their respective techniques. The participants were members of these dance companies.

These three events allowed Martha to think of the class as a theater experience, and her demonstrations began to resemble a great dance. She always spoke in terms of the theater and the need for projection and awareness of self.

Today, as the added dimension of the spiral is emphasized in the training, the demands for even more awareness of the internal movements of the torso are necessary. A dramatic richness is apparent in the movement and one is conscious of the fulfillment of Martha's vision: to move fully, to explore fearlessly, and to demand the potential that is in each of us. Indeed, for Martha Graham, "dancers are the acrobats of God."

ANNA SOKOLOW

Anna Sokolow was a member of the Graham company from 1930–1938. She formed her own company in 1931, and has worked extensively for the Mexican Ministry of Fine Arts since 1939 where she introduced modern dance. She has also been instrumental in the formation of modern dance in Israel with her work for the Inbal Dance Theatre. In addition to choreographing for her company, the Player's Project, Sokolow has created dances for the Broadway theater, the Joffrey Ballet, the Netherlands Dans Theatre, the Alvin Ailey American Dance Theater, and other companies. She has taught in colleges, universities, and major acting studios, and is a longtime faculty member of the Juilliard School in New York City. In 1962, Sokolow received a Dance Magazine *Award. In 1989, she staged her work,* Rooms, *for the Israeli government in remembrance of the Holocaust. In 1991, she received the Samuel H. Scripps American Dance Festival Award for lifetime achievement in dance.*

I will always remember how I met Martha Graham and Louis Horst. I was a student at the Neighborhood Playhouse when it was on Grand Street in New York City. It was a theater and a school for dancing when I enrolled. It was a revelation for me to be introduced to Martha Graham and Louis Horst as teachers at the Playhouse. At a very young age, I knew that what I wanted to do was dance, and to make dance an art form that would express the way I felt about things.

This great woman then introduced me to her techniques— rather, to her way of moving the body—and it had a very great effect upon me. Another revelation occurred when Louis Horst taught me choreography. We students didn't even know how to spell the word, let alone know the meaning of the word. In his quiet, subdued, but strong way, he explained what choreography was and why it was important for dancers of our generation to learn it and become creators. The combination of Graham and Horst brought forth our creativity. Because I felt the impact of their teaching and trusted them, I learned a great deal.

At that time, it was an introduction to another world, for not even ballet was as popular as it is today. It was so important to have Graham teaching us her way of movement, it was so interesting and so deep, and it helped me find my own way of expression—but that happened at a later time.

It was all a tremendous and overwhelming experience. Being in her early works, such as *Primitive Mysteries* and *Celebration*, showed us the wide aspects of her art, and what her way of moving could express. The impression on me was so profound that I will never, never forget what she has taught me.

I feel that Louis Horst is not mentioned frequently enough as an influence in modern dance choreography. Although he is honored for his teaching, it was the *way* he taught and how he encouraged us all that was so important. For instance, he taught us music by making us analyze a form such as a pavane. He would instruct us in the history of the pavane, and explain its place in society, encourage us to construct a dance in that context, and then to construct a dance based upon what the dance inspired in us within the structure, form, and meaning of the pavane. These classes continued once a week until we had a thorough knowledge of music and gained the ability to analyze a score—something I don't believe our choreographers today know how to do.

Not only are choreographers today insufficiently schooled in music, they lack a general cultural knowledge concerning the arts in all their forms. They have little or nothing to say, and although this may be a general condition of our society at the present time and common to all the arts, it is not a theatrical experience, nor a dance experience, to present oneself on stage and indulge in acting out one's own meager ideas that have no meaning to anyone else.

Another thing I do not like to see is modern dancers insert badly performed ballet into their works, such as a poorly executed *attitude*, an *arabesque*, or a careless beat. I saw the Ballet Russe de Monte Carlo when that company first came to America in the 1930s, and I loved it. It was good dancing. Although there were whisperings in the dressing room that we should not talk about or see ballet, the visiting companies were wonderful to see. That did not apply to the local groups that were so bad, there was nothing to learn from them at all.

Primitive Mysteries, which I mentioned earlier, was the work that led me toward what I wanted to do—create religious dances. I left the Graham company to do just that, and Martha showed me the path I needed to follow. I was schooled and disciplined in her technique, but that was not my main interest, and, after that, although her influence will never leave me, I found my own way. The Mexicans, with whom I have worked for so many years, call me "the rebel with discipline." I could not be more pleased with any description of myself than that.

DOROTHY BIRD

Dorothy Bird was a member of the Graham company from 1931–1937. A kiss from Pavlova helped her decide to dance as a career. In the summer of 1930, Bird left her family home in Western Canada to study with Martha Graham at the Cornish School in Seattle. Bird also demonstrated for Graham in classes and lectures.

After leaving the Graham company, Bird danced in Broadway shows for Agnes de Mille, Helen Tamiris, and Jack Cole. She returned to modern dance in the José Limón Trio under the direction of Doris Humphrey, then back to show business for Eugene Loring, Jerome Robbins, Anna Sokolow, and Herbert Ross. Bird has taught at the School of American Ballet, at the Neighborhood Playhouse for twenty-five years, and in schools throughout the New York metropolitan area. She was dance consultant for the Nassau County Office of Performing Arts and created the Nassau County Dance Ensemble. Dorothy Bird Villard now lives in Merrick, New York.

It was in Seattle, in the summer of 1930, that I first met Martha Graham. She came for the entire summer as an artist-in-residence to choreograph and teach at the Cornish School. I'll never forget how she walked into the school's large, airy studio, brushed aside all introductions and said, "We've no time for formalities. We have a lot of work that we are going to do together this summer. And you may call me Martha."

This was a shock because the head of the school was known as Miss Aunt Nellie. It was a different time. You can't imagine how startling this was. Then she smiled and said, "I have something very exciting that I want to share with you. I have just come from dancing the role of the Chosen One in *Le Sacre du Printemps* (by Léonide Massine) on the great stage of the Metropolitan Opera in New York City. I discovered something as I stood still for a long period of time in the work with the dancers all around me. I learned how to command the stage while standing absolutely still. And I'm going to teach you how to do that.''

It was almost magical. With this promise, she distracted us from the fact that she had closed the door on the Fifth Position, *port de bras*, pointing the feet, and, like Isadora Duncan, had turned her back on tutus, pointe shoes, tiny jeweled crowns, and little white wings. She was prepared to go much further than Isadora. Martha warned us of the dangers of big, romantic passions. Out went all the small, delicate, sentimental themes and the last ripples of the Delsarte System* that Ted Shawn had been teaching with such devotion in the Denishawn School. All of this went into the compost pot. Along with this went the stories that can be told in words. Martha said, ''Dance has nothing to do with what you can tell in words. It has to do with actions, colored by deep inarticulate feelings that can only be expressed in movement.'' She did not permit a single sentence, neither a subject nor an object to be considered as a basis for a movement, only verbs and adverbs. Those were the only words she had in her notebook at that time. (Graham always made a script for her movements and works in a notebook.)

We did not for one instant question the strict discipline that Martha Graham imposed on the range of movement patterns that were gradually being introduced to us. First, she broke down the movement into its smallest particles and showed it to us. Together we examined it and learned the source of its initiation. Then she explored ways of putting the particles together again in designs and patterns infused with high levels of energy. If I were to tell you that she was an absolutely incandescent teacher at the time, it would be only words. But it was a fact that she set the students on fire; it was unbelievable.

Martha selected five dancers and was working with us to create phrases of movement for the dance interludes in the Greek

---

* François Delsarte (1811–1871) was a teacher of singing and declamation, and a founder of a system of gesture and movement based upon his observations of the laws of expression. Ted Shawn was a student of the movement and wrote a small book in 1963 on Delsarte, *Every Little Movement*, reprinted by Dance Horizons.

play, *Seven Against Thebes,* that was to be presented at the end of the summer. She used the classroom to experiment and to create exercises that fed into the choreography. She was always engaged in the process of exploring, eliminating, and simplifying in order to capture the appropriate qualities of movement for this very inexperienced group that came from various parts of the country: Alaska, California, and me from a one-room schoolhouse in Canada. She used every possible image and device to awaken our imagination including thousands of animal images—images I never heard her use later.

I continued my studies with Graham at Bennington College from 1934–1938. Bennington was a marvelous experience because we had food—meals were supplied—and there was the outdoors.

Martha only allowed us music that I considered a thump! She had this idea that the body must carry the melody and the pianist would play only one note many times, then go to another note. The pianist would beg to be released from this tedious job, but the movement had such flow it needed no more support. The sound just punctuated it.

We didn't turn much at this point, but there were two turners, Marie Marchowsky and Bonnie Bird. Each of us had our own special quality. All I think I did was go up and down!

The leaps and runs were not as big as the splits you see today, that was a long time in coming. We always did the side extension leaning forward.

We did barrel turns, like Russian folk dancers, and falls: done on a breath, suspended, held, and performed on the count of four up, four down; then on three. It was based upon a faint. Coming up was on a breath. There were tilting falls. Some people were really able to suspend out and fall marvelously.

SOPHIE MASLOW

Sophie Maslow joined the Martha Graham Dance Company in 1931 and remained until 1944. Her training began at the Neighborhood Playhouse with Martha Graham, Louis Horst (in composition), Nanette Charise (ballet), and Muriel Stuart (from the School of American Ballet). Maslow has since choreographed over 100 works for her own company, the New York City Opera, the Israeli Batsheva and Bat-Dor Dance Companies, the Harkness Ballet, and many other groups. She has also created works for the many colleges and universities where she has taught, as well as works for television and theater. She has been a judge on arts councils, and in 1984 received an honorary doctorate from Skidmore College. Maslow is copresident of the New Dance Group Studio in New York City where she continues to teach and choreograph.

When Martha Graham came to the Neighborhood Playhouse, where I was a student, she had already developed her basic movements and the theory of how to train a dancer and a dancer's body to become an expressive instrument. It was a way of expanding the expressiveness of dance so that it could reflect everything in human life—or almost everything in human experience.

In the many years that I was in the company, it never occurred to me to look in a dictionary to find the meaning of contraction and release. I looked it up just recently, and although there are many definitions of the word, down at the bottom of the list a *contraction* is defined as ''a basic movement in modern dance.'' So, we have made *Webster's Dictionary!*

I was in the same class as Anna [Sokolow] at the Playhouse and found it as inspiring to work with Martha and Louis Horst as she did. Even though I was an adolescent, I felt that everything Martha was doing was right. We didn't turnout our legs. (That meant nothing to me since I never studied ballet.) All of her movements were meaningful. Martha gave everything imagery or a meaning to guide the quality of the movement, or we found a meaning for ourselves in everything. Other kinds of dance became unimportant to me.

I remember sitting on the lawn with students at Bennington College in the thirties talking about the "dance of the future." We could feel life changing around us and new things happening in the arts, and we wanted to be part of that future.

I've chosen a few movements that we performed at the time to illustrate how deceptively simple they seem to be. They are performed in the center. The first movements are called *lifts* and are comparable to the opening *pliés* in a ballet class. The feet are parallel; there is a rise to the half-pointe and a slow descent. The torso is balanced over the feet. The contraction and release principle was included in different positions going down to a *grand plié*—sitting on the heels. These were very broad movements done in an adagio tempo. Some of the variations alternated between parallel and turned-out legs. These movements require control and balance. It was hard to hold the movement and keep it smooth. It had to be pure and clear. Every part of the body was used so that when you finished the series, you were warmed up. Properly done, they are beautiful to see. The body was used in a spiral position, as well; the hands were cupped and the arms straight, or easy, as the series progressed.

Then there was a series I secretly used to call "the revolutionary étude" because it gave me the image of someone standing on top of a hill and calling people to action. The tempo is as for a march and the quality of the movement should be very percussive. This is a series of bounces, or rebounds from heel to half-pointe with an emphasis on the up movements. It involves leaning over as if you were talking down to a group of people somewhere on the floor. You turn to the side at times. The *élevés*, or rises, were continuous; continuous movement is what produced the strength and stamina in the dancer, and the series tightened the buttocks as well. Unfortunately, this series is no longer taught, because I feel it added a quality of movement as it developed strength. It was abrupt and heroic in quality and broadened the texture of positive movements.

Turns were learned in a sequence that includes a preparation, a half rotation or turn, and a full turn. The eyes do not "spot" as in turns in ballet, and the body moving from low to high positions forms the turn. The body begins in a tipped position parallel to the floor in *attitude* (one leg bent at the knee and raised to 90 degrees). The force for the turn is gained by the lift of the torso and a twist in the back—the spiral—that makes the body turn.

The head floats around with the body, as do the arms. The arm opposite the lifted leg is raised, then the arms open to the side. From the *attitude* position, the pivot occurs when the body is raised and the lifted foot is placed on the floor. This movement can occur without a turn, as in a preparation, or in a half- or full-turn series. The tempo is a slow four counts.

Executed across the floor on a horizontal plane, this turn was performed with a half rotation or a full rotation. As the *attitude* leg is placed on the floor, the supporting leg shifts the weight of the body and frees itself to do a swooping 90 degree *rond de jambe* toward the direction of the horizontal series. The body, when the crest of the *rond de jambe* in back is reached, pivots to face the direction of the series and the *rond de jambe* leg steps forward to begin the next turn in the series.

I don't remember turns included in our early classes, but I do remember turns in our early group dances performed in concerts without Martha participating in the dance. *Course* was one of the names I remember for a concert dance with turns.

Pitch turns with a straight raised leg usually come from a low contraction. The turn is strong and the position kept parallel in the body; often this was performed as a full turn. The first appearance of this turn, I believe, was in *Deaths and Entrances* (1943).

Walks were another deceptively simple part of the class, especially for dancers now, when they do them, because they are turned-out. It's harder now to teach a simple, straight, graceful smooth walk than it used to be. I used this walk in my early dances, one of them was *Folksay* (1942), and I found it difficult for the dancers to learn.

It is a simple walk but must carry life within it and not become boring. It was taught in a circle and was continuous. From the moment the foot is placed on the floor, the thigh and knee straighten and the other leg moves into the next forward step. It is almost like pushing into a strong wind with a straight torso, or like bravely facing a storm in a peaceful way. The movement goes into the waist, which means that the hip has to be over the foot of the forward leg. It is a beautiful stride with the torso erect and the back leg lengthened without exaggeration.

The walk is performed in 4/4 time and begun slowly, each step taking four counts; then two counts; and finally taking only one count. Triplets on one count and other variations complete the series. It all has to flow.

Walking may sound like an easy and natural thing to do, but it is not easy for dancers. Then, again, there are so many different kinds of walks depending upon the characterization of the role. For instance, in my ballet *Champion* (1948), it was very hard for dancers to walk like fighters who have sunken chests and protective, rounded arms. It took hours of practice!

Leaps were done with the lifted leg in back bent at the knee, the bottom of the foot facing the ceiling. Height was the objective. Usually, the leaps were performed as "run, run, leap," in a 4/4 tempo, but sometimes they were performed as a leap on every count with the accent on the crest of the movement.

Some of these things are done today with too much lightness. Dancers have spectacular technique and can do just about anything, but it seems to be less meaningful because they employ no weight in the movement. They are not interesting movements when they are just tossed off.

The differences between dancers of my generation and those of today are in their reasons for dancing. I studied at a time when we chose the way we wanted to dance. No one earned a living dancing, aside from a few dancers in Broadway shows. So we could make our own choice as to how we would dance. It was not a question of what jobs were available and what was right for us individually. It was a matter of what was right for dance. We didn't want to be embarrassed by being in poor productions. It was better not to work.

But in Martha's works, not only was the movement important to me, but her philosophy as well. She seemed to feel the pulse of the time—the anger, sharpness, aggression in life at that time—things that were part of our lives, and she seemed to be able to put those things into an art form and communicate them.

I feel today's dancers find a place for themselves that is "right for them," rather than where dance is heading in their time and place.

LILY MEHLMAN

Lily Mehlman was a Graham dancer from 1931–1936. She began dancing at the age of seven. She came to the Graham studio when she was sixteen and shortly afterwards became a member of the company. She was in the group that performed with Graham as the Chosen One in Le Sacre du Printemps, *in the first American presentation choreographed by Léonide Massine after the Nijinsky version.*

Mehlman was also in the opening program at the Radio City Music Hall when the Graham company played the first bill. She became a choreographer for the WPA (Works Projects Administration) dance and theater division and later choreographed for ARTEF, a Jewish theatrical company.

Mehlman taught extensively at her own studio and at children's schools, and performed with her own group. In 1935, she received the Dance Magazine *Award for performing the outstanding solo of the year. In 1958, Mehlman moved to Los Angeles where she became involved in dance therapy at UCLA, later working as a dance therapist at General Hospital and at Mount Sinai Hospital in New York in a closed ward for disturbed children. She worked with adolescents at Gracie Square Psychiatric Hospital in New York and the Kennedy School for Retarded Children.*

In remembering the performance of *Le Sacre du Printemps*, staged by Massine with Martha as the Chosen One, I recall that they worked very well together. We, in the group, never saw a rehearsal between them, but somehow, in an odd way, they understood one another. The rest of us just followed what we were told to do, sometimes with difficulty because we didn't move that way. But we managed.

Martha was so extraordinary and so beautiful in that solo that I remember when she finished there was a stunned gasp from the audience.

I remember her leaping around the group as she was going into the center for the sacrifice. Her hair was flying, her legs were high in the air, she was flying. There was so much power, so much strength and beauty, you could not help but become mesmerized. We, in the group, were transfixed and wondered what she would do next. She would lift her arms, and turn her head in such a different way from the ballet movements.

Graham's *The Rite of Spring* (1984) was different from Massine's folkdance quality. The men moved in ponderous ways. Martha's *Rite* had force but entirely lacked folk material, although there were groups of villagers that partook in the ritual in a more abstract way.

MAY O'DONNELL

May O'Donnell was a member of the Graham company from 1932–1938, and rejoined the group in 1943–1953. Born in Sacramento, California, the young O'Donnell studied with Leila Maple, then Estelle Reed, a student of Mary Wigman in Germany.

She learned the Graham technique in New York at the Graham school and soon joined the company. Between seasons, O'Donnell spent six summers with the Graham group in Bennington, Vermont. Between 1938–1944, O'Donnell taught in California and created her own works. World War II and the inactivity of dance in California brought her back to New York in 1944. Following her return, O'Donnell was asked by Graham to rejoin the company and, while continuing her own dance activities, she participated in the creation and performance of major roles in Graham's new works of that period. O'Donnell received guest artist billing.

O'Donnell's active career has spanned from 1932–1988 as a performer, choreographer, and teacher. Her technique is taught in several colleges and schools, and her works are performed by a number of companies.

I had seen Mary Wigman's work in a concert in San Francisco about 1930 or so and liked it very much. She was on a sensational tour of the United States. A student of hers in San Francisco knew there was a world beyond ballet and Michio Ito so I began to study with her—Estelle Reed. Someone saw me perform and recommended that I go to New York to work with a dancer I didn't know—Martha Graham.

I studied at the Wigman School when I got to New York. The school was sponsored by Sol Hurok, the impresario. It was in Steinway Hall on 57th Street between Sixth and Seventh Avenues, and it was crowded. The teacher was Fé Ahlff, a big, beautiful Germanic person. The class was more an experience than a lesson. Ahlff would start off with her Oriental drums (there was a big Oriental influence in Europe at that time—even Wigman wore what seemed to be a Nautch [Indian] costume with its circular skirt and bare midriff bodice). Fé would do some kind of step and the rest of us, like blind mice, would follow. She never looked back at us. When she reached the end of the room, with us following, she'd return to the original place and cross the floor again adding a little variation to the movement. It was like a theme-and-variation process. I found it interesting and fun.

One day, I was asked to be in a class that Wigman was going to watch. It was a class in improvisation; I had no idea what that meant. I was very shy and bothered by the whole idea and by the whole class as I observed people doing what I thought was improvising. It looked wild with dancers doing odd movements and making funny sounds to get attention; so I just left.

I finished taking classes because I had paid for them and went to classes by Graham. I recognized in Martha someone who had a technique, and that it was something I would have to hang on to.

Martha's school was on 9th Street between University Place and Broadway on the parlor floor of a brownstone. The classes were so crowded that there was no room to move anywhere but in your own space. We did *stretches* and *lifts*, things that required that you push into your body to find the roots of the movement. It was highly concentrated and if you weren't strong enough, the work didn't look right. There was a lot of work in opposition—one part of the body working against another part. Tension, contraction, and release were taught. There were *backfalls*—those long stretches in the thighs that took strength—*brushes*, and *prances*. The attitude at that time was: "Return to the primitive—down with anything decorative; it's a tough world out there." The entire art world was searching for new ways to express itself in art, architecture, music—all to the same call. Henry Cowell had a series called "New Music," and Charles Ives, Carl Ruggles, and Edgard Varèse were on the scene making new things happen in music.

Compared to the popularity of the Wigman School uptown run by Hanya Holm, the atmosphere in the Graham school seemed more personal. We had direct contact with Martha who taught the class.

Very soon after I began to study, Martha took me aside and asked me to study with Gertrude Shurr, one of her teachers, with the goal of my joining her group. That idea seemed made in heaven to me. It was about 1932, I believe.

When the school moved to 66 Fifth Avenue, in 1933 or 1934, the larger space permitted us to move across the floor in low walks, to run in place, and take long strides in place with many variations in the counts and in direction; it was a continuous and widening series.

Prances were practiced as a lift between the raising of the knees, so that the movement was very ''up.'' That movement was later used in *American Document* (1938), and we also did *triplets* in a down-up-up rhythm with the heavier accent on the first step and lighter accents on the second and third steps. We also did *running steps,* they looked like a small leap, in two counts: down, up (heavy, light); then in a slower tempo: heavy, one, one, one. These became bigger and bigger as a logical result.

Extensions evolved in the course of her discovering what new shapes and images could be created with the body. The same extensions were done with the body held in a horizontal position as in a standing position with the working knee and the supporting leg parallel to each other. *Falls* onto the shoulder took control, opened into a release, and, with a swing of the legs, the torso came up. But the falls to the back were performed by few in the class. I did them, and I think I had more control than most because I had more strength. My knee-to-hip bone is long and that permitted me to arch and lean backwards from a standing or kneeling position and to hold my balance with the support of a strong back.

I remember one piece in which I was in the center doing this long, slow fall backwards while everyone else was running around me. It was torture! But Martha liked the contrast of one slow movement against the swift movements of the group in this dance. She gave me credit on the program for it. She was always generous in giving credit to her dancers. The only way I can describe it technically is to compare it to a craftsman working with metal to find the tension between two points. In the body, the fall took such a high release that you had to calculate the tension between the knees and upper back in order to sustain the movement for a long time.*

My relationship with Martha was good but not a terribly personal one. She liked me because I worked hard. I had to. It was so difficult for me to get to New York; I just had to make it as a dancer.

During rehearsals I watched Martha search within herself. Some of the dancers became annoyed when she changed steps during the next rehearsal, but I liked to see the progress in the changes, in the molding of the work. Going with her into her search taught you a great deal about yourself. You could discover where your base was, that point within yourself where your energy is released into movement and dance.

In the early 1930s, the time of the Depression and social unrest, Martha created dances of social content that expressed the protest, anguish, frustration, and mood of the times—the angularity, the dynamic intensity, the beat of her body rhythms and movements, the search for the return to the primitive, were all part of this time. Martha could sense those things and in her dances she gave voice to these tensions and feelings that attracted an eager and responsive audience.

The first new dance that I was in was *Chorus of Youth—Companions* (1932). She spent hours trying to break away from the primitive and find more freedom, and, at the same time, keep some depth. I don't remember that she demonstrated very much. She'd do something, then get us to do it. If you made her movement look alive, made something out of it, it had value for her. We could contribute to Martha's work in that sense, not the actual steps, but in the working out of the quality she wanted.

A much more open work was *Celebration* (1934), a work with which we began concerts. It was sensational because we never stopped jumping except for a short section when we were on the floor. The audience loved it and I think it was a breakthrough. When it was reconstructed in 1977, we got Lily Mehlman, Marjorie Mazia, Anita Alvarez, Gertrude Schurr, Ethel Butler, Marie Marchowsky, Kathleen Slagle, and me together. Bonnie Bird was in England and Anna Sokolow couldn't come. Jane Dudley came

---

* This backfall occurs in *Chronicle* (1936), which was about the Spanish Civil War, in a section called "Steps in the Street."

from England. The reconstructed version of the work combined all of our memories of how it was originally danced.

In the late 1930s, Martha's creative drive began to unfold in new ways that gave greater range to her dance technique and movement vocabulary and brought more lyricism and freedom into her work.

At Bennington, Martha had done *Panorama* (1935) that had many of the elements she was trying to capture. It culminated in *American Document* (1938) as an abstract piece but with a reference point, and led to *Letter to the World* (1940), a piece of Americana—the new phase. *Document,* for which my husband, Ray Green, wrote the music, was a full, major work. The main sections of the dance were in episodes—Indian, Puritan, Emancipation, and Declaration—all touching and creating an atmosphere that captured the spirit of a growing young nation in its struggle to find identity on the way to modern times. It was the American scene.

Although other choreographers such as Lew Christensen, Agnes de Mille, and Eugene Loring were doing dance works on American themes, these works leaned toward ballet vocabulary, while Martha kept the modern dance vocabulary and used movements in a unique and innovative way.

In 1938, *American Document* ended my time with Martha as a student and member of her group. I married composer Ray Green and returned to San Francisco to explore and develop and find my own way in dance.

For Martha, *American Document* was the beginning of a new phase in her life and work. It was the first time that she used a male dancer, Erick Hawkins. This led to new directions and challenges.

In 1944, I returned to New York to establish a studio with Gertrude Shurr and to carry on my own work. Following my return, Martha asked me to rejoin her company to do important major roles. It was with concern that I agreed because I did not want to disrupt my own direction. But I decided to try to work with her and carry on my activities at the same time.

Although I did not take classes in her technique and could only spend limited time in her studio, I could feel that the atmosphere had changed when men entered the company. The men weren't as docile as the ladies. For Martha, the work became full of characterizations and relationships. It was a larger palette.

You could also see that the dancers in the company in the 1940s had, in most cases, some previous dance training, especially in ballet. Pearl Lang, Ethel Winter, and Yuriko had more facility because of their ballet training and Martha liked it very much. It gave her a greater range, and it seemed to me that the contemporary modern dancer who had—and has today—some ballet training, who has the capacity to absorb the modern dance spirit, can bring an ease to the performance in any company. Martha was able to imprint or plant her stamp on these dancers and have the quality of Graham emerge.

When I returned to the company in 1944, I took over special roles in Martha's current works, but soon was involved in new dances in which I could contribute in an important and creative way. Most of my rehearsals were with her alone. She would map out the work and say, "May, this is your music," and I would know exactly what I would be doing in relationship to Martha or to the other dancers in the work. She encouraged me to use my own intuitive imagination and spirit because we had a great sense of rapport. It wasn't a question of knowing her technique, but rather being able to sense what role of compassion I was to play based upon her role. I knew how to move accordingly. My original role in *Appalachian Spring* (1944) was stimulating and gratifying to me for that reason. It was different from the thirties when everything was set.

I felt that my role as the Pioneer Woman in *Appalachian Spring* represented a strong, outward, visionary kind of pioneer spirit from which the American nation was founded. It was endurance over hardships and an eternal spirit. Martha never mentioned this to me but said something like "May, do you want me to work with you or would you like to feel it out?" I said I would try something that she might like, but if not, naturally, it would come out of the piece. We had, later, when the piece was played, a kind of interplay that was wonderful. You just did what came out of the moment, although you still did the same steps.

I originated the secondary role in her *Hérodiade* (1944) in the same way. Once I knew what my character represented, I could keep it in the right relationship. Martha never explained things, you had to create from your own imagination. I developed the Handmaiden role as a simple, devoted, and compassionate figure who helped her prepare for what might be her destruction, trying to protect her from going into the unknown which might mean death. It was a psychological relationship.

The Chorus in *Cave of the Heart* (1946) was another role created by me, so to speak. There was a story in this work, but it was again a question of relationships. I had to know where Erick, Yuriko, and Martha herself were onstage, and, like a chess game, it had to work that way. It almost dictated itself.

Dark Meadow came along in 1946. I think I sort of balanced off the tensions in her works when she created them. She could make everyone shake and shiver until she exploded. I was called "She of the Ground," or the Earth. I think she thought of me that way.

Eventually, the demands of my own work made it impossible for me to give so much time to Martha.

My final appearances were in *Hérodiade.* In 1953, after an interval of two years, Martha called me once again to perform this work with her. I knew that it would be our last dance together, but I also knew that it would be a beautiful way to part.

MARIE MARCHOWSKY

Marie Marchowsky, a Graham dancer from 1934–1940 and then again in 1944, began her study at the Graham school at the age of thirteen. In 1931, she joined Anna Sokolow's first company, The Dance Unit. After leaving the Graham company, Marchowsky created her own group in New York and taught extensively. In 1969, she moved to Los Angeles to head the dance department at the California Institute of Technology, and created a dance company and school of her own. Marchowsky then created a dance company and school in Toronto, as well as becoming principal of the Toronto Dance Theater School.

Marchowsky returned to New York to teach at the City College dance department. Although she is retired, she continues to take class and maintains an active interest in dance affairs.

My first contact with the Graham movement was in 1930 through Lily Mehlman, my dance counselor at camp and a member of the Martha Graham Dance Company. She was the catalyst for my entry into the new world of dance.

I continued to study with Lily after returning home from camp and learned that Martha was giving a concert at the Craig Theater in the West 50s. I was determined to go, and my mother arranged to take me. It was an overwhelming experience. I saw four group works: *Primitive Mysteries, Heretic, Bacchanale,* and *Moment Rustica,* and three of Martha's solos, *Two Primitive Canticles, Adolescence,* and *Harlequinade.*

After seeing the concert, my one desire was to study with this great woman. I discussed the possibilities with Lily and learned that there were no children in Martha's class, but she offered to speak with Martha about me. A few week's later, I was told that I may take a class with Martha with the warning that if I did not behave like an adult, I would have to leave. I was elated, and needless to say, never uttered a word in class for three years. I later learned that Martha told the women in class to refrain from mentioning sex in the dressing room when I was present!

The movement at that time was considerably different from that of today. The early thirties was a time of searching and exploration, the discarding of the old and the creating of new forms of expression. It was a time of upheaval in all the arts.

Martha's technique reflected this explosion. The movement was percussive; stripped to the bone; unadorned; dark; dramatic; and never decorative. This new path brought a new meaning to dance as it delved into the fundamentals of movement. With her vision, Martha created an art form that was unique and independent of any dance that had existed before.

Class began with floorwork but was cursory compared with the floorwork of today. The fundamental source was in the contraction and release principle, with the pelvis as the central motivating force. The exercises were primitive: legs and feet parallel, hands cupped; feet flexed as if rooted into the earth. The movement was influenced by American Indian dances—a source of inspiration to Martha.

Following this period, a development in the technique evolved from the culture and mythology of ancient Greece in which the Dionysian rites were center stage. While the movements retained their primitive quality, the body stance was locked and altered into a two-dimensional image resembling figures in a Greek frieze. Extensive exercises were created with the body in this archaic position. The classes also incorporated great body swings or tilts that had an abandoned and fearless quality with hard-hitting body contractions powerful enough to propel one across the floor. A great variety of falls were included: backfalls in a spiral; side falls; and falls from a tilt that would send one sliding across the floor. These wonderful falls have remained in the technique to this day.

In general, the classes seemed to be built on more horizontal than vertical lines. In moving across the floor, as in walking or running, the body had to appear to be pushing through a heavy mass, much like the pressure confronted when walking through water. Forcing through a mass, using the pressure in space, made for great intensity and drama when traveling across the floor.

In the midst of all the ladies was Louis Horst, Martha's mentor. His teaching of dance composition was responsible for our development as artists. Studying with him was like going to a school of higher education. He was an integral part of the studio. There were times when Martha was too tired to conduct rehearsals and Louis would take over. What a disciplinarian he was! He'd sit at the piano, smoking his cigar, and, although his hooded eyes appeared to be closed, he didn't miss a thing. His caustic comments on our performance could be formidable. We called him "Eagle Eye." Louis's contribution, as the composer for Martha's early works, was unique. At that time, Martha created her dances without music, and when completed, Louis would watch the dance, record the counts, and return with a score that fit splendidly. He was a pillar of support; a man dedicated to the development and growth of modern dance.

Each year, movements were added to the classes as the experimentation and exploration continued. I believe it was in 1933 when a new set of exercises were added to the technique. Based upon the seated-Fourth Position (sitting on the floor), the upper body moved around the spine as if in a spiral. This innovation was the root from which flowered the extensive and rich vocabulary that embraces the floorwork of today. Some of these early innovations can be seen in the dance *Celebration*, particularly in the movements that were on the floor. I recall the working title as "Energio," or energies, and the dance lived up to the title. It was the first time I was present when Martha choreographed a work. In the previous years, jumping and leaping played a minor role in the technique. But *Celebration* called for a great deal of jumping and we had to learn to use our feet from positions mostly flexed to mostly pointed in order to jump.

This dance, choreographed for the twelve women in the company, was a departure in that its core was composed of jumping—eight to ten minutes of it. It was a tour de force that left us all breathless. We had been rehearsing the dance in sections until, one day, Martha suggested we run it straight through. It turned out to be an exercise in sheer physical endurance and we all felt slightly ill at the end. Eventually, we were able to take this physical challenge in stride.

All the costumes Martha designed were ingenious in their simplicity and were as if wedded to the dance. The wool jersey or stretch fabrics she used sculpted the body. She designed the costumes on us as she cut the fabric and pinned us into them. As the night wore on and she continued to pin, one was lucky if the pins didn't prick too often.

Much of the vocabulary introduced in the class was the result of movements created for each new work. Thus the technique was consistently growing and expanding. In the works Martha created for herself and the company, the group was antagonist to her protagonist. The group was used as a mass in an opposing force. Including men in the company added a new dimension. The men were no longer part of a mass but emerged as individual players in the dances. The movements became more lyrical, decorative, and formalized.

III

The Postwar Years

The Graham company was revolutionized by the introduction of a new element in the early 1940s: Erick Hawkins. Hawkins, who was Graham's husband, served as a catalyst for an entirely new approach to dance. Harvard-educated, trained in ballet, and a member of two of the fledgling Balanchine ballet companies of the thirties, Hawkins introduced a new philosophical and aesthetic bent to the Graham company.

Hawkins first met Graham at the legendary Bennington summer school of dance in the late thirties; his encounter with her led to a repudiation of his ballet training, although his first job as a member of Graham's company was to teach ballet movement to the company members. Some of the more radical members were shocked to see a ballet barre brought into the Graham studio; for them, ballet was the enemy, representing an outmoded form of movement that was antithetical to everything the modernists were trying to achieve. But Graham was far more interested in the movement possibilities that ballet offered to be bound by convention.

Through the late forties, Hawkins originated a number of memorable roles in Graham's works, including "Every Soul Is a Circus" (1939), Letter to the World (1940), Appalachian Spring (1944), Cave of the Heart (1946), and Diversion of Angels (1948). Other male dancers were introduced into the company, notably the talented Merce Cunningham in the forties and Paul Taylor in the mid-fifties. The increased dramatic possibilities of using men in the company deepened Graham's interest in psychodrama, the eternal struggle between men and women as it is portrayed in myth.

The impact on the classes was great. While the basic class was well-established in the thirties, a new emphasis on the dramatic began to show itself in the work. The introduction of ballet techniques helped the dancers hone their skills while expanding their movement vocabulary. Graham's introduction of men into the company, along with her selection of a new generation of women, led to a greater emphasis on physical speed, precise lifts, and greater overall virtuosity in the company.

JANE DUDLEY

*Jane Dudley joined the Graham company in 1935 after
studying four years with Hanya Holm at the Mary Wigman School in New York. She was with the Graham
company until 1946, then returned in 1953 and 1970.
From 1938–1952, Dudley choreographed and performed
with Sophie Maslow and William Bales in their Trio
Group; was Graham's teaching assistant at the Neighborhood Playhouse School of the Theatre; and was a
charter member with Graham, Humphrey, Limón,
Maslow, and Bales of the American Dance Festival held
at Connecticut College. In the 1960s, Dudley was a
member of the faculty at Bennington College, and at
the invitation of Graham, became artistic director of the
Batsheva Dance Company in Israel. In 1970, she was
appointed vice-president and senior teacher at the London School of Contemporary Dance, where she continues
to work today. She has choreographed extensively in
the US and the UK, where a videotape of her concert
"Young Dancers" has been widely distributed.*

Martha came to the studio on 56th Street, on the top floor, where
I used to study. I was sixteen and saw her coming up the stairs
with her long hair and looking very shy. I said to myself, "That's
Martha Graham!" I had seen her in concerts—the ones in the
late twenties when she did performances entirely as solos. There
was no company, not even The Trio when she first began. If you
can imagine a concert of thirteen or fourteen solo dances, performed with the most extraordinary movement imagination and
originality, and with the most beautiful and proper costumes,
with lighting—all created by Martha—you can imagine what a

deep experience it was to see. And it was just that for me. And an inspiring one.

I remember once dancing the *Brahms Waltzes* for Ruth St. Denis. After I danced, she came up to me and said: "You know, you're exactly Martha Graham." It must have been my long dark hair because I can't imagine doing *Brahms Waltzes* and being like Martha Graham!

I had also seen two classes that Martha taught at the Neighborhood Playhouse to young actors in the late twenties: the studio was then on Madison Avenue. The young actors were doing a contraction, tilting back and holding the heels, turning into a high arch and returning to the original position about three times, then rising, all holding onto their heels! There are not many dancers who can do that today with control. Martha was uncompromising and put them through a grueling but invaluable experience.

Martha had a class of about twelve women in that 56th Street studio. I watched them doing a sequence that started on the back, proceeded to a lift in a contraction (by the way, I've given up that term because it has become hard to convince a modern dancer's body to do it; I call it a rounded back). I saw Martha do this lift, raise one leg and rise to a standing position, then, still holding the raised leg, lower to the floor and back to the original position. That takes immense strength and control. Her natural facility for movement was so special and so original it made her technique exceptional.

ERICK HAWKINS

Erick Hawkins was born in Trinidad, Colorado and studied with Harald Kreutzberg and at the School of American Ballet in New York City. He danced in Balanchine's opera ballets staged for the Metropolitan Opera in the early 1930s, and was a charter member of Ballet Caravan performing in works by Eugene Loring and Lew Christensen.

He attended the Bennington College summer workshop in 1936 and joined the Graham company in 1938 where he remained until 1950. (He was married to Martha Graham during this time.)

In the 1940s, Hawkins formed his own company with which he continues to choreograph and perform. The repertoire of the company is extensive and it continues to travel throughout the world. Hawkins has a school in New York City.

I was in Balanchine's first *Serenade* (1934) when it was performed by students of the School of American Ballet at the Felix M. Warburg estate in White Plains, New York.

Lincoln [Kirstein] later asked me to do a second piece, called *Showpiece*, for his Ballet Caravan company formed in 1936. The company was to encourage American dancers, choreographers, composers, and designers. It toured for three years and included works by Lew Christensen, William Dollar, Eugene Loring, and me. Ballet Caravan was to appear at the First International Dance Festival in New York City—one night of ballet, one night of modern dance. That is where I first met Martha Graham; she appeared on the modern dance night.

Lincoln gave me a very short time to do the second work, only three weeks. The theme of the piece was the Minotaur, later used by Christensen, and even later, by Martha for *Errand into the Maze* (1947). But before that, I knew that there was a new world of dance coming. I had read about Isadora Duncan in *Theatre Arts Monthly*, a beautiful publication. I felt that, in order to do this piece as a metaphor on the theme, and because I wanted to respond to this new world of dance, that I would need more time. It was not suitable to use old, standard movements for such a mysterious theme. Lincoln understood and gave me tuition to study at Bennington College where Graham, Humphrey, Weidman, and Holm were teaching in 1936. I was convinced that I had to find my own way. The boy from Colorado did not fit into the Balanchine mold, which, at that time, was closer to St. Petersburg than the American Ballet that it became. I took Martha's summer course. In a way, I think it was Balanchine's advice to me that provided some impetus for me to search for myself. When I asked him if I could be a dancer, he said, "You can't tell what you can do until you do it." I took that as a challenge that opened doors for me to do whatever I wanted.

So, Martha's course, drilled into me by Ethel Butler at that pivotal time in my development, opened doors and expanded my awareness of freedom. I don't remember any men in the class—Merce [Cunningham] came along the second year I was in the company in 1939. My new path melded with Martha's and I think I brought additional energy and expanded the use of her movements in her dances.

As an example, in *Night Journey* (1947), in the lifts, it was natural for me to participate in working them out since I was the active participant in the work. And in *Appalachian Spring* (1944), in the role of the Husbandman, and in other works, I made some participatory contribution.

But you see, since we were all trained in the same way, the source being the center of the body, any small contribution was valid to the work. From that same source, I developed my own way—from the center. I'm sorry to say that in some of the Graham students I see today, that principle seems to be lost.

Losses, such as a center, I feel are the cause of so many injuries today. If your theoretical and practical use of the body is correct, you won't do a bad movement that might cause injury. The body can be driven, but it has to be within the bounds of the capacity of the student, and be accumulative, and observing of the laws of movement—the skeletal limits. I've had a long career as a performer, because I developed correctly and gained stamina slowly.

The training in the classroom at that time was well established and I don't think that anything from the ballets found their way into the classroom. There may have been an excerpt from the repertoire given, but that is not basic to the principles of her training. It's true that I taught ballet at the suggestion of Martha Hill that second year at Bennington because that is what I knew, but I don't think it had much influence on the basic training. The floorwork that Martha introduced was a tremendous contribution to dance: no weight on the legs; control from the center. Weight and center are serious concepts. Wouldn't it be nice if dancers today could embody both the current concept of lightness *and* weight, using one or the other as the work demanded it? "Gravity is the root of grace," is a saying by Simone Weil that I remember as a suitable image for dance.

I think what I really contributed to Martha is what you might call an aesthetic. She was a great artist and I don't see the great artist in performance—the moving, overpowering presence—in dancers today. Perhaps that's because of a general deterioration in the arts. The motives have changed. An aesthetic vision has to be present—a desirable goal that is not based upon gaining notoriety, money, or acceptability—but is based upon reaching that aesthetic vision. That doesn't mean starving, but it does mean that a group or a dancer has to have a standard, a level, a goal that is beyond the demands of the general culture.

There is a lot of competition in dance, so many more people in dance than ever before, and not a great deal of good judgment in the people who make dance possible. Razz-ma-tazz has found an audience. People are doing a dance for the wrong reasons. I think our generation danced because we had only one reason: the desire to dance to an aesthetic goal. That was satisfaction enough. I'm not talking about art for art's sake, but about being honest in the reasons for dancing and for creating dances. It's a concept I keep in mind, trusting that the result will be fresh and from innocence. It takes a clean palette every time. And it wasn't created to please anybody. There is no dance that I have done that I'm ashamed of.

In 1950, Martha created *Eye of Anguish* on the theme of King Lear for me. It was not successful. It was performed only once in Europe and dropped for the last time. I think it failed as a piece because Martha could not enter into that character of Lear as she had in female characters. Martha thought through a work using her psyche, her emotions, but I don't think she could do it for a leading male role.

But that was an honest failure. It was dropped. That's what I mean by honest. If a work is not up to the highest standards, it should not appear on stage. We've got to stop accepting compromises.

JEAN ERDMAN

Jean Erdman was a member of the Graham company in the years 1938–1945, 1970, and 1974–1976. Her vigorous initiation into the company required that she learn four works in ten days before a Boston performance.

Between the times of her return to the Graham company, Erdman made a solo world tour in 1955. She developed a "total theater" approach for The Coach with Six Insides, *based upon James Joyce's* Finnegan's Wake *(1962), which won a Vernon Rice and Obie Award. She has been an artist-in-residence in arts festivals throughout the United States, Europe, and Japan.*

As a choreographer, Erdman has worked for the Repertory Theater of Lincoln Center, the Vivian Beaumont Theatre, and the New York Shakespeare Festival winning the Drama Desk Acting Award and a Tony nomination. In 1972, with her late husband, the noted author/philosopher Joseph Campbell, she founded the Theater of the Open Eye in New York City, and continued to direct numerous total theater works. In 1985, she was commissioned jointly by the government of Greece and the US State Department to create an evening of theater works for the Athens Festival, "Myth and Man Symposium," at the Herodes Atticus Theater. She is currently creating a video archive of her early repertoire. Erdman lives in Honolulu and in New York City.

When I was a student at Sarah Lawrence College, I had my very first dance lesson with Martha Graham and was transported. I knew, just by the way Martha put her feet apart and squatted into an open *plié,* that she had the key to dance and to life itself. Her inspiration never left me.

I grew up in Hawaii knowing only Isadora Duncan and hula dancing, so the revelation of the tremendous intensity of expression unleashed by the body as I saw it in Graham's work was totally new to me. It was an experience just to watch it.

As a student at Sarah Lawrence, we had the privilege of having Martha's dancers come to teach us once a week—either Ethel Butler, May O'Donnell, Bonnie Bird, Dorothy Bird, or Martha herself. It was wonderful to get into that beautiful world.

Martha by that time—before 1938, when I joined the company—had a company of females who loved what she did and found it sufficient. When I was invited to join the company, upon arrival at the studio, I found that I had to learn four dances in ten days prior to my first performance in Boston: *Celebration* (1934), *Heretic* (1929), the Act of Judgment section from *American Provincials* (1934), and a new piece, *American Lyric* (1937), with music by Alex North. In *American Lyric,* as the title suggests, we did some of the turns with a leg in somewhat of an *attitude* position.

It was a terrifying experience because Martha said to me: "Oh, you're so much taller than I thought you were!" and then placed me with Jane Dudley and Sophie Maslow, her experienced dancers. But that may have been lucky because people would watch them instead of me, I thought.

The only thing I can remember about that performance is that during those four counts toward the end of *Celebration,* when I could stop jumping and breathe, I saw stars—the only time in my life that I saw stars from sheer exhaustion! But I was forever more involved in the meaning, the message, and the physicality of Martha's art.

The following year, she invited a young man to come into the company for a new piece called *American Document* (1938). She asked Erick Hawkins to dance in the work and another young man, an actor, to do the narration. It was the first time she included a male dancer. She kept the style as it was, but gave Erick stronger movements to do and we performed it all over the country on tour.

Then, she said to us one day, you're going to study ballet with Erick. At that time, we wore only bathing suits, no tights, and no shoes for class. Barres came into the classroom, and shoes.

It was incredibly difficult to move our legs without a torso movement. Martha began to incorporate movements that kept the body still and used the turnout, but were not balletic.

These involved a different problem of balancing and centering without impulse from the center that was so basic to Martha's technique and expressivity. They were incorporated into turns, and I remember that it was very difficult to add that new dimension to the technique. It seems so simple now, but it was innovative at the time.

Martha began to be interested in drama. Here was a man and a woman, a relationship of male and female present on stage. The arms came into greater play, and the movements had more flow. But never, never was that powerful center lost; that meaning of her vision. When she choreographed *Letter to the World* (1940), what it meant to dance as a female came into the creating and performing of the work. We found it strange to do what we had never done, but it was all part of the experience of being in her company, learning what she wanted us to do, learning who we were, learning what life was about, and what the art of dance can be.

MARK RYDER

Mark Ryder was a member of the Graham company from 1941–1949, and made his debut in the premiere of Letter to the World *(1940). In 1950, he and Emily Frankel debuted as the Dance Drama Duo which became, in 1954, the Dance Drama Company. In addition to their own choreography, they commissioned works by Valerie Bettis, Todd Bolender, Sophie Maslow, Zachary Solov, and Charles Weidman, and performed throughout the US until 1958. Ryder directed the Jewish Community Center of Cleveland from 1961–1965; was on the faculty at Goddard College in Vermont (1966–1973); and from 1974 to his retirement in 1988, was an associate professor of dance at the University of Maryland at College Park.*

When I became a member of the Graham company, the tradition was already a strong movement, but my entrance into the company followed a different pattern from the other dancers.

I lived in New York City and studied in the childrens' classes at the Neighborhood Playhouse when it was on Madison Avenue. I was the only boy in the class for five years! Then, I studied ballet, took other modern dance classes, and studied with Marie Marchowsky before going into the senior classes at the Neighborhood Playhouse. It was in these classes that I studied with Martha and Jane Dudley. It all seemed a natural and logical development of my past study. It didn't seem exceptional—that was just how it was.

When Martha needed a man in *Letter to the World* (1940), it seemed natural to be chosen—after all, why shouldn't she chose me, I thought. That's the point I'm trying to make—that if you were a man and coming into the school or the Playhouse at that time, you were spoiled rotten. Boy, was I spoiled. I expected things to come my way and they did.

I do have two small insights to offer on Graham's technique: One deals with the "fall on four"; the second deals with the change in the makeup of the women in the Graham company, beginning in 1941, and how this change affected the technique.

When I arrived in the Graham studio, the "fall on four" (the count of four) was taught only to the left side. When I was trained, symmetry was an article of faith. Turns were done on both sides, extensions were done on both sides, so were the leaps, and combinations, as well. You were taught to do things on the right side and also on the left.

Martha pulled some totally unexpected rabbits out of her intuitive hat in many rehearsals. She showed me how strong a tool intuition can be—especially for geniuses. I saw her stuck, at a dead end, in a piece of choreography from which no logical development was possible. Then, blip: We'd see another miracle from her. It was always the right movement at the right moment, but seemed to come from nowhere. It made it difficult to contradict her. She might be wrong, but how can you argue with someone who always seems to be doing the right thing at the right time! How could she have been wrong about falls to the left in her choreography?

She not only used our bodies, she also used our inner lives, she co-opted our souls.

I observed a change in the bodies of the women in the company beginning in 1941. The women of the group seemed big-boned, robust. Jane Dudley, Sophie Maslow, Jean Erdman, Frieda Flier, Ethel Butler, and Pearl Lang seemed to fit in with them. I left in 1943 for the army and returned in 1945 only to find Yuriko, Helen McGehee, Ethel Winter, and Pearl Lang (who had dropped ten or fifteen pounds) and several others, along with the larger women. The basic character of the company seemed to have changed and with it, the technique. What had been slow and powerful became lightening fast, like quicksilver. If you were to compare the group in *Primitive Mysteries* to the Chorus in *Night Journey*, it would be clear to see the contrast of style in the techniques used in each.

Postwar, I took classes with Yuriko, Marjorie Mazia Guthrie (who was the wife of Woody Guthrie and the mother of Arlo Guthrie), and, perhaps because I was out of shape, everything seemed so much quicker. I couldn't get all the steps into the combinations anymore. The smaller bodies moved more quickly. The tempos seemed changed.

I wondered if this was Martha's design, or if it was because of the new crop of dancers who were smaller in comparison, or whether everyone was smaller, slighter, and skinnier. I think it was Martha who had changed her aesthetic at that time in an intuitive move to reflect society's swifter, sleeker, expanding world.

HELEN McGEHEE

Helen McGehee was a member of the Martha Graham Dance Company from 1944–1972, and a principal dancer from 1948. She has been a choreographer, designer of theatrical costumes, director of her own company, lecturer, teacher, and author of Helen McGehee, Dance, *and* To Be a Dancer, *her most recent book. She currently lives in Virginia.*

Martha Graham's creativeness is the body and soul of her technique. Her search deep within herself to objectify in terms of movement the inner life of the character to be portrayed brought discovery of movements that she then needed to teach to her dancers. Because she was so gifted with a rare, naturally talented body, she could execute and consequently demand that the dancers also execute remarkably difficult and different movements. These movements required range, skill, and incredible strength. We, as dancers, and especially as teachers, must always be aware of this source.

A technique for dancing should not solely be concerned with developing bodily skills. But dancing should be a source of commanding a deep, inner energy. The dancer has a responsibility to be vivid. In a lifetime of dancing—performing—there will be times when a dancer will feel that she cannot do what is asked of her. Illness, fatigue, and distress can make it difficult to summon up the energy needed to make a performance live again. This is why your technical training and your preparation for a role must have always been so thorough and so constant that you will know how to go about rekindling this life.

Technique is the means by which you rekindle this vitality. For this reason, the dancer must never allow herself to make a meaningless movement—one that lacks concentration.

Actually, I'm talking about how one goes about the business of taking class. Try to become totally concentrated on what you are doing; aware; without practicing carelessness; and do nothing by rote. In this way, dance technique can bridge the gap between exercising and performing on stage.

I was fortunate, during my early development, to have had so many classes taught by Martha herself. I remember her saying so often, "You have so little time to be born to the instant." We, from experience, knew that this was true. My generation had fewer opportunities to perform than today's dancers. Therefore, I always felt the need to take class as an act of ritual, a commitment to the theater.

The more concentration you are able to bring to bear upon your object, your role, and your images for the role, the more likely that inner energy and vividness will be released at the precise moment you perform the role. The frustration of dance as an art form is that it exists only at the moment of performance.

Martha taught me that, to make theater, every component is essential. Everything is important. No aspect is secondary. Theater requires the commitment of each person involved working to the utmost of his or her capacity to produce that rarity that is excitement. She made each of her dancers realize that the devotion to the performance, to the work itself, rather than to your own importance, makes the piece ring true, and also makes it work successfully for you.

This is something that must be truly believed. It cannot be faked or it comes across as false. Nothing is more destructive than competition; both to the work of art and to the competitor.

I feel lucky to have been involved in so many Graham productions that offer the rare, almost unique, opportunity to experience this kind of participation; the creation of an experience greater than the sum of its parts that makes it such a deeply joyous thing to do.

We all know about the contraction and release, the breathing of the body, but what is less frequently taught and emphasized is another element—suspension. It is the moment of hanging there between the two elements: the moment of balance before the change. Without this suspension, the breathing becomes forced, positional, and mere huffing and puffing.

Techniques for performing are discovered through experience, through doing, and in all probability, will differ with each personality. For me, the flow of energy must be toward the performer during the act. You must be so charged that you have power to pull energy from the audience. For this reason, I find it dangerous to watch other performers immediately before performing myself because I need time for the flow to change direction. In Act I of *Clytemnestra*, after my exit as Electra, I could always enjoy Linda Hodes' Cassandra and Ethel Winter's Helen of Troy.

You must be strong enough to admit vulnerability. You are exposed on stage. The reason for being on stage is precisely this exposure. Exposure is what you are communicating, and your protection is your preparation.

Apropos of vulnerability, Martha would sometimes say: "Let the skin be like the skin of a grape." This was meant to allow ease and release of tension.

After a recovery from a fall, she would say: "Let a gentle waterfall flow down the body."

I have collected during the years with Martha what you might call "tips" for performing. One such tip is about marking (performing a rehearsal or any activity without the use of full energy): "Don't! If you must, then mark the physical movement but keep intensely the dramatic meaning. Never mark that. And keep the true timing and musicality of the role. Always be involved with what you are intending."

Another tip concerns energy. Frequently, in class, when obviously the class energy must have been low, she would have us do a simple sequence of movement with an added vibration, such as *heel ripples* or fast, soundless clapping of the hands, which, of necessity, would demand energy to be built up in the body to be released consequently into a more difficult movement. For example, on four counts, a simple circular walk using a vibration of the hands on the first two movements released into a wide turn on the third, and recontained into the walk on the fourth step. The most demanding use of this vibration is when Medea draws the snake from her increasingly vibrating body.

Another tip is about touching. In *Appalachian Spring*, when the Followers make a picture of adoration around the Preacher, we were to look as if we were touching him, but were not literally to do so. The image would project farther without actual touching, and the energy required to hold the position would make the image more vivid. In *Night Journey*, the Daughters of Night should give the *feeling* of tearing their clothes, but not literally do so. That literalness, suddenly, would make it all too mundane.

The tremendous joy of performing lies in the opportunity to be so many different kinds of characters. The danger in the dance world is to lose variety. I feel there is so much emphasis on the extraordinary, on the splashy, and on the overextended, that there is not enough contrast through the use of restraint and composure. Consequently, the spectator becomes sated with bravura and the point is lost.

One of my favorite roles in the Graham repertoire was Artemis in *Phaedra* (1962). It was wonderful simply to stand there simply being.

I need to withdraw and become quiet before performing. I need to feel at home in the theater, and I like to be there at least two hours before curtain. Part of this quieting takes place during the ritual of makeup. The other ritual of preparation is warming up. We see changes in the technique over the decades, because dance is a living organism and therefore subject to change; without change it will die.

I feel that many of the changes of detail wrought, for example, in some basic technical sequences are a result of Graham's desire to get at the unteachable. She swings the pendulum back and forth in order to have the dancers experience the excitement of equilibrium at the center. The center cannot be exaggerated, as, of course, the extremes can. Her search is for the beautiful, the unteachable, but nevertheless discoverable center.

Thus, we find Martha's work still expressing continuity with the past, but with the past as now the living present.

©1990 by Editions Heraclita. From *To Be a Dancer* by Helen McGehee. Used by permission.

JOHN BUTLER

John Butler was a member of the Graham company from 1943–1953. He was born in Memphis, Tennessee and attended the University of Mississippi. As a performer Butler appeared in the original Broadway production of Oklahoma! *(de Mille) in 1943 and in* On the Town *(Robbins).*

He has had a long and notable career as a choreographer for television on Camera Three (CBS), the Bell Telephone Hour (NBC), and for WNET (now PBS). In addition, he created works for Gian Carlo Menotti including Amahl and the Night Visitors *and* The Unicorn, The Gorgon and The Manticore *(later performed by the New York City Ballet) for the Spoleto Festivals.*

In 1955, he founded the John Butler Dance Theatre and continued to choreograph works for the Metropolitan Opera Ballet, Nederlands Dans Theater, Pennsylvania Ballet, and the Harkness Ballet. Carmina Burana, *created in 1962 and performed at the City Center Theater, won him high praise and the* Dance Magazine *Award in 1965. He continues to choreograph and stage his works for companies throughout the world.*

History is just a series of daily things. It was not possible for us to know that we were making history by being in the Graham company. We felt that we were doing something new and exciting and we really didn't care what anyone else thought about it.

Martha had a sense of humor when she taught movement. For instance: I had a basset hound named Camille (named by Greta Garbo, to whom I gave private dance lessons at one time).

I would leave Camille with Martha when I went on my various tours, because she loved Camille. He would lift his great head and stretch as hounds will do. When he demonstrated this to a class that Martha had brought him to, she said: "This is how your throat should look when you bend backwards!" Her humor was dry, and sometimes very naughty.

We had a relationship, a private friendship, outside of the professional one. I regard it now as having been almost a mystical one. Maybe it was because we were both Irish and had a sense of mystery about things. She was a sorceress, you know— in the Irish sense of having insight and being able to command people to do her bidding. She had superhuman power.

I remember something superhuman occurring after the breakup of her marriage to Erick Hawkins. I was the last one to leave a rehearsal one night and went into the studio to bid her goodnight. I heard her sobbing. But it wasn't the crying of someone in grief or despair—it was something deeper, almost like a wounded animal in pain. Their was a torrent of tears, and her body was wracked with tension. It was extraordinary, like something from a Gothic tale or a Greek tragedy. I sat there for about two hours until her body calmed down and I felt I could leave. It was not a human incident, but mythic.

I had come straight from Mississippi to New York—green, and probably the only boy in the state at the time who ever thought about dancing. I was practically stoned out of the state. My background was ballet and ballroom dance and I taught successfully in New York, but I knew that was not what I wanted to do.

One day, in a bookshop, I saw photos of Martha by Barbara Morgan. Only in youth can you have the kind of arrogance I had to look her up in the telephone book and go to her studio.

I said to the receptionist: "I'd like to meet Miss Graham, please." Everyone within hearing distance was horrified. They buzzed around and finally Martha emerged. I said: "I would like to work for you, Miss Graham." "Come back tomorrow morning," she said, in her wisdom, "before the class," knowing that if I didn't show up, I was not worth the bother.

I showed up in my prince outfit. Since I was the only boy who danced, I was everybody's prince in Mississippi high-school performances. I got into my baby-blue tights and doublet—my baby-blue outfit. You can imagine what an impression I was making on her. I flew around the studio in my rotten Mississippi ballet steps until she could stand it no longer. "Sit down, young man," she commanded. I stayed for the class. It was two hours long, but I knew instantly that it was what I wanted. At that time, the movements were still percussive, strongly rhythmic, and not yet romantic. Later, when I rejoined the company several times, the movements became more lyrical.

Years later, when Martha and I had become close friends, she would sometimes look at me across a dining table and say, "Hello, prince."

The first year I went to her classes, Martha also sent me to the School of American Ballet. It was very strange. Here I was the Graham boy going uptown to the 59th Street and Madison Avenue SAB and wearing ballet slippers in class. I think she just wanted to see my body rid of the bad ballet I had been taught in the past. It lasted for two or three years with Muriel Stuart as my teacher—Stuart had studied briefly with Martha. Muriel put me on an egg-custard diet. Honestly, I was so innocent and trusting and so enchanted by these important and famous ladies, I would have done anything they said in order to dance.

Graham classes were not painful for me because I had ballet classes early in my life and because I was a dedicated tennis player. I had stamina.

When we became close friends, telling each other confidences, and aside from the great woman that she was, I saw her vulnerable and sensitive side. We shared feelings about our private lives, almost as if it were a secret relationship. To me, it was sacred, and whenever I was interviewed, I never gave away any of her private thoughts.

In the studio, working with her on a role, no one else existed for you or for her. She was the enchantress in this situation. Captivated by her, you were caught completely. Half of the time, I didn't know what the hell she was talking about—it was so mystical and spiritual—way out of my Southern range. But somehow, it got to me on the level of dance, and I moved as she wanted me to.

There were those in the company to whom she entrusted participation in the creation of roles. They used her language, but she guided them and respected their contribution when it

was right. It may be for this reason that so many of her dancers
became choreographers. They knew the process that she showed
them, and as a result, but not intentionally, they became independent of her.

Something I could never understand, however, concerned
her use of music. While I am so influenced and responsive to
music, I find it still a mystery that she was not. The pieces of
a dance she would rehearse in a studio and then commission
a composer who prepared the accompaniment to that section
in another place. It would all fit at some point, but I never could
understand how or why. As always, she wrote the libretto for
the entire dance, and Samuel Barber, or Gian Carlo Menotti, or
whoever, appeared to be utterly baffled when it was put together
and it all seemed to work. Even if Martha decided to do her
slowest passages to their liveliest sections, the contrast matched
the libretto as an underlying or underscoring of the intent.

What I learned from her, and from all of this, was pure theater. I responded more to her sense of drama than to her movements. I never had a great technique. She was so articulate, and
had a capacity for such diverse imagery, that I learned from her
how to get to the dramatic moment with honesty, brevity, and
clarity, just as she did.

When she directed you, she reached into your being to get
the strength she knew you had. You always grew with her.
That's the reason I kept coming back to perform in the company
between my own seasons and commissions.

From some of the dancers, she called forth their physical
capacities, but from me, she called forth drama and theater.

Working with her was a double act of faith. She trusted you
with her theater and you gave it back to her. You had to reach
her plateau; she demanded nothing less. In turn, you found
yourself making the same demands of others when you were
entrusted to direct them. The legacy is handed down in this way.
It is a sacred trust that works on sacred ground.

Martha would come to my early concerts and give me comments. It was something I valued. When I had my big success
with *Carmina Burana* (1962) at the City Center Theater, I took Martha home, as I always did, after the performance.

She kissed me long and hard when we parted and said:

''Now, I tell you goodbye.'' I was no longer the pupil. Not her equal, but now on my own path. She never came to another performance.

IV

Work with Actors

One area of Graham's career that is not as well-known is her landmark work with actors. Since 1928, she was on the faculty of the Neighborhood Playhouse, an important center for dramatic training in New York. Graham and members of her school's faculty have taught hundreds of actors basic principles of movement. Some of the very first actors to benefit from working with Graham were Bette Davis, Blanche Yurke, Gertrude Lawrence, and director Ruben Mamoulian. The list of distinguished alumni includes: Gregory Peck; Joanne Woodward; Tony Randall; Robert Duvall; Lorne Greene; Eli Wallach; Amanda Plummer; Woody Allen; Mason Adams; James Caan; Suzanne Pleshette; Diane Keaton; Patrick O'Neal; Jo Van Fleet; Darren McGavin; Efrem Zimbalist, Jr.; Tammy Grimes; Anne Jackson; and Tyrone Power.

Graham simplified her basic movement techniques in order to give actors a basic dance class. In turn, she showed actors how movement could define character. Rather than working from the inside out, as the famous Stanislavsky Method did, Graham emphasized working from the outside (the movement) in (the emotion). Movement could define emotion more economically than words.

In addition to this contribution to acting training, Graham choreographed and even directed plays during her early years at the Playhouse. Much of this important part of her dance legacy is undocumented.

ANNE JACKSON

Anne Jackson, like Graham, was born in Allegheny, Pennsylvania. She attended classes with Graham at the Neighborhood Playhouse from 1943–1944. In 1948, she attended Lee Strasberg's acting technique classes at the Actor's Studio along with James Dean, Shelly Winters, and Marlon Brando. She also studied acting with Herbert Berghof and Sanford Meisner.

As an actor she is best known for her numerous stage performances, including: Anya in The Cherry Orchard, *Nellie in* Summer and Smoke, *Luka in* Arms and the Man, *Laura in* The Glass Menagerie, *and Daisy in* Rhinoceros. *She recently appeared with her husband Eli Wallach in the 1991 Chicago production of* Love Letters.

In the 1950s she was among the pioneering Broadway stage actors who brought theater to television viewers through major network series such as Goodyear Playhouse on NBC; GE Television on CBS; and Armstrong Circle Theatre on NBC. She has appeared in films and on television throughout her career including: The Journey *(1959),* Lovers and Other Strangers *(1970), and* Marcus Welby, MD *(1972). She received the* Village Voice's *OBIE Award for her performance in* The Typist *and* The Tiger.

I don't know how the photographs of Albert Einstein, Eleanora Duse, and Martha Graham happened to be put together on my dressing table. It was a happy accident. I keep the grouping because it seems so right and because I've grown accustomed to seeing them daily. They inspire me. I like what they stand for: simplicity, truth, beauty, and hard work.

Duse and Einstein are long gone; Graham was the youngest genius in the group, and lived the longest. She was someone I could marvel at and tell her so, a living reminder that the spirit can soar long after the body is defeated by gravity.

Yet Martha was an acquired taste. In the beginning I didn't know what all the fuss was about (being green and uneducated). When I met Martha at the Neighborhood Playhouse in 1943, she was well over fifty. I was fresh out of high school. My idea of a dancer was Eleanor Powell.

I had read a quotation from a critic on seeing Graham and her modern dancing: "I expected," he said, "Miss Graham to give birth to a cube." That description certainly seemed apt. I thought she was arty and eccentric.

All of those contractions and percussive movements her disciples put us through, the endless *pliés* and stretches on the floor—the barre work made us groan. I liked the pony trotting, the leaps, and the running; I didn't like the long black jersey tubes we wore for demonstration—but once dressed in one, the feel of the jersey sent my body into motion and I would clown around, do runs and falls in an imitation of Martha for my classmates.

We were usually drilled by one of her dancers; Martha came on rare occasions, like a general inspecting the ranks. When she entered the studio, our backs grew straighter; even the walls got whiter and the mirrors seemed to gleam.

I think I came under her spell after a rather silly incident. She was getting us ready for a student performance and cracking the whip. I was not on the beat, I guess, and she slapped me on my rump with force because, she said, I was not giving my all. I went wild and ran to the door. "I'm telling Mrs. Morganthau on you!" I shouted, and raced straight into the administrator's office. Mrs. Morganthau was a dear chubby little lady with cheeks like a squirrel's. She adored Martha and, I suspect, was terrified of her. She had given me a scholarship to the school and I felt justified in coming to her with my complaint. When I blurted out my indignation at being hit, her cheeks puffed up in alarm.

"Oh dear," she said, "don't waste a moment; go back and apologize to Martha at once."

I rejoined the class. Nothing was said, but there was a silent understanding between us. My imitations after that grew less and less frequent. I tried harder to execute the leaps and falls and make them my own.

I came completely under her spell when my friend and classmate Lucille Paton said, "You better learn your contractions, Annie; Martha said if you don't you'll never get a man."

The man I got [Eli Wallach] was also influenced by the high priestess. Martha had locked horns with him and then won his heart several years earlier. "Eli," she ordered, "walk, walk as though you carry the seed."

What sent my heart racing was her eloquence, her passion about dance: "There is a vitality, a life force and energy, a quickening which is translated into action — and because there is only one of you in all time, this expression is unique. And if you block it, it will never exist through any other medium and will be lost. The world will not have it."

DOUGLAS WATSON

Douglas Watson performed in the Graham company in 1946, a suitable preparation for his continuous work until his recent death. As an actor, he was the recipient of the 1973 New York Drama Desk Acting Award, the New York Critics' Variety *Acting Award, the Clarence Derwent Acting Award, the Theater World Award, and a best actor Emmy Award for three years running.*

Although he might be best known as MacCory in NBC TV's Another World, *Watson played Don Parritt in O'Neill's* The Iceman Cometh, *and later, Eben in* Desire Under the Elms. *He was Romeo to Olivia de Havilland's Juliet; the clerk in T. S. Eliot's* The Confidential Clerk, *Henry VIII in* A Man for All Seasons, *and appeared with Jennifer Jones, Eva Gabor, Ruth Gordon, Katherine Cornell, Helen Hayes, Julie Harris, Judith Anderson, and Margaret Leighton in stage plays.*

I am not a dancer, and have never been. So I will speak from a little different viewpoint.

On the other hand, I guess I was a dancer for about six months in 1946. After World War II, I came to New York to study acting—I had studied acting earlier. I had six hundred dollars—my wife had the other six hundred dollars—and with two children we lived with my parents. I had come to New York to make a fortune as an actor.

The first thing I did was enroll in a Martha Graham class. Why? I'll never know. It was the apex of my experience in theater as I think it should be. I've done about thirty-five or thirty-six plays in New York, but the high point of my career was in those few months with Martha.

When I enrolled in that class, because there weren't many men around after World War II, I was offered a place in the company for the Broadway season that year. It was the year Martha choreographed *Dark Meadow* (1946). I had never danced professionally but had had classes since I studied with Maria Ouspenskaya, who had a Graham student teaching movement for her.

I wasn't allowed at times to come out onto the floor in the studio because the cracks on the bottom of my feet were so deep that I would bleed on the floor. The classes were very intensive, but also very rewarding.

I would just like to say what the Graham technique has meant to me as an actor. Graham recommended me to Katherine Cornell, a leading actress in the 1940s. I got the role of Eros, a small part in *Antony and Cleopatra*. In the play, at one point, Antony, defeated in battle, turns his back to his swordbearer, Eros, and says: "Kill me. I don't want to be shamed by being brought before Octavius Caesar in his triumph." So, Eros draws the sword to kill Antony, but loving him so much, he can't do it. While Antony's back is toward him, Eros says: "Are your ready?" Antony answers: "Now, Eros." But Eros plunges the sword into himself. This, mind you, was my first Broadway production and others in small parts in that production were Tony Randall, Charlton Heston, Joseph Weisman, and a few others who are now famous.

I heard them say behind my back: "What is he doing! He's dancing the part, for God's sake." And indeed I was. To me, the greatest performer in the theater was Martha Graham so I was doing Martha Graham.

So this is what I did, of course, I tamed it down, but not too much, by the time the show opened. I was into the basics. There were two basics I followed—the contraction and the extension with the fall. Don't think I still don't do these exercises every day at the gym!

I would just like to say briefly what Graham meant to me psychologically. The Method, which you probably all have heard about, was taught by Maria Ouspenskaya, who was a member of the Stanislavsky troupe, and who was left here because Americans wanted to learn it. The Method, simply put, is to get the insides going so the outsides will do other things. You prepare your character's history; you think a lot; rev yourself up emotionally. What I learned when I came to Graham was that the external can create the internal, rather than the internal creating the external.

An example of how I applied this to acting can be seen in *Richard III,* the night scene. Richard says: "Guilty, guilty, guilty," because he kept killing people and needed punishment and someone who could stand up against him, which no one could do until the end when Richmond is successful. His grandmother, in the play, describes him as a "touchy, wayward" boy of five or six years old with a humpback. I think he had a right to be a little touchy. I took it that the physical disability was an externalization of what was going on inside of him, and took place in the course of the years before the play and then to some extent afterwards. (I interpose here that what Graham did for me was enable me to externalize the warmest passions I have within myself that are covered up by societal behavior. She puts this skeleton on the outside, not on the inside, whereas, as in Chekhov, one never talks about what is going on inside, it's all in the subplot. You know what I mean, you are supposed to shoot the billiard ball into the second corner and it means your heart is breaking.)

In Shakespeare, everything is said, and sometimes more than needs to be said. He puts it all on the outside, into the action in front of you. And this is what Graham does so well.

TED DALBOTTEN

Ted Dalbotten studied with Martha Graham at the Neighborhood Playhouse School of the Theatre in 1946–1948. He danced in the Nina Fonaroff and Sin Cha Hong companies. Dalbotten was Graham's accompanist at the Neighborhood Playhouse, 1948–1953. For the past five years, he has taught the music classes at the Martha Graham School of Contemporary Dance. He has been an adjunct faculty member of Columbia Teachers' College dance education department since 1969, and continues at the Neighborhood Playhouse as an accompanist.

I have never taught the Graham technique. I studied with Graham at the Neighborhood Playhouse and then played for her classes there for the next five years. I have three things to share with you; one of them deals with what might be called an innovation; the others are about various aspects of her teaching.

I can't place an exact date on what I'd like to relate first. It didn't occur to me at the time to run home and write it down, but my guess is that it was around 1950.

Martha taught both first and second year classes at the Playhouse. One day, when the first-year class had finished the floorwork, but before Martha had brought them up to a standing position, she walked over to a short section of barre next to the piano, turned and faced the class and began talking about ballet. She spoke about its long theatrical tradition, how its technique had evolved over a long period of time, and added some other things as well.

Then, she put her right hand very delicately on the barre and said: "There is something the ballet has known for many years. It is called Fifth Position." She carefully brought her left foot in front of her right foot into an absolutely turned-out Fifth Position. "And," she added, "I think we can find it useful." Thereupon she lowered her eyes and proceeded to do a perfectly placed *plié* in Fifth. I imagine that Fifth Position had made its appearance at the studio shortly before this, but I wouldn't have known about it.

I took Martha's second-year acting class at the Playhouse in the forties and fifties. Martha spent a period of time with us on speeches from Shakespeare. There was one basic approach she used—there were variations on it, but this was typical.

Martha would hold each of us across her lap as in a Pietà position where we would go into a very deep contraction—and if it wasn't deep enough, you can be sure that Martha saw to the necessary adjustment. Then she would have us turn our heads to the side giving the position additional dramatic tension, but also releasing the throat so that we would be able to speak more easily. And in this seemingly unlikely pose we would perform our speeches. But two rather startling things occurred if the student used his breath fully in that position: First, there was a tremendous sense of urgency and communication; second, and even more astonishingly, voices that often were habitually breathy suddenly became vibrant and full with a deep sound. And, for the first time for some of the students, the girls sounded like women and the boys sounded like men.

Martha always claimed that she knew nothing about voice production, and, from a scientific point of view, she may not have. But she arrived at a startlingly effective result that neither the speech nor the singing department had been able to duplicate.

I think that many young people who have never seen Martha herself perform think of her work as being exclusively a serious and ecstatic exploration—as she herself has put it—of the deep matters of the heart. But Martha has a sense of humor second to none. And she was a marvelous comedienne.

I remember her using this aspect of her personality one day—but for a very serious purpose. One day at the beginning of an initial first-year class at the Playhouse (you have to remember that most young people entering the school forty years ago had never taken a dance class in their lives—nor had heard of Martha, for that matter), she gathered the students together at the far end of the studio. She talked to them in her magical way about the formidable physical skill that theatrical performance demands; of the theater artist's responsibility to astonish and delight; and of how the work must seem effortless although it might be grueling, and must give the effect of spontaneity. As she talked, she did a *développé* with her right leg into a fabulous side extension (although she was now in her mid-fifties). And the leg stayed up there as she kept talking. She didn't acknowledge it, but continued to talk as if nothing out of the ordinary was happening. Of course, by now she had all the students completely mesmerized, including the male unbelievers. Then for the first and only time, she barely glanced at her foot as if to say condescendingly: "You may come down now." And down it came.

I was sitting at the piano and my impulse was to applaud this delicious bit of theatrics. But I didn't because Martha had demonstrated this piece of virtuosity for a very serious purpose. She was presenting to these neophytes a glimpse of a kind of theater that most of them didn't know existed. And she was playing for high stakes—for their allegiance to that theatrical vision she was describing.

Both she and that vision have had my allegiance for a very long time.

BERTRAM ROSS

Bertram Ross performed with the Martha Graham Dance company from 1949–1973, as Graham's partner and leading dancer. He was a participating creator in most of his thirty-five starring roles. In addition to performing, Ross was Graham's demonstrator from the fifties through the seventies, and appeared in several films of Graham dances.

Ross pursued an active theater career after leaving the Graham company and appeared in several dramas and musical revues, and choreographed several shows as well. Most notably, in recent years, Ross created An Evening with Bertram Ross *and another cabaret act,* Wallowitch & Ross. *In this act, he has appeared in New York City, San Francisco, Washington, DC, Los Angeles, and Palm Beach.*

Martha's teaching was rich in imagery. It was a fantastic experience demonstrating for Martha. I was her demonstrator in the fifties, sixties, and seventies. I think she did her best teaching at the Neighborhood Playhouse.

At the Playhouse, she used all sorts of imaginative devices to get the actors to move. The Graham technique itself is inherently dramatic and theatrical: in working with actors, Martha found ways to make the point of each exercise vivid and meaningful, and extremely clear and specific. Sometimes she was so taken with the results she was getting with actors, that she would use her discoveries back in her own studio, which made the studio classes that much richer.

Demonstrating for Martha at the Neighborhood Playhouse was a revelation. Classes at the Playhouse were only one-hour long, as opposed to the one-and-a-half-hour classes in her studio. Martha managed to keep the class moving, say all the brilliantly wonderful things she had to say, cover all the basic Graham exercises (floorwork, center, and traveling) and make corrections, all in the space of sixty minutes.

In the fifties and sixties, in order to teach at Martha's studio, the prospective teacher would be required to demonstrate for Martha for about a year. Bob Cohan, Ethel Winter, Helen McGehee, and Mary Hinkson all demonstrated for Martha. I came after them. I used to say that I was "The Last of the Red Hot Demonstrators."

It was during Martha's years at the Juilliard School that things began to change. Martha was teaching in the same building that Anthony Tudor and Margaret Craske were teaching in. It was almost as if Martha was intimidated by them, and didn't want them to observe what she was doing, as if she didn't have faith in her technique when compared to ballet. Anthony Tudor said to me later "I liked her old technique better. So, people hurt their knees! But it was more inventive, it was more exciting!" Many of the exercises with parallel legs began to disappear. Certain floor exercises were also removed because Martha felt that "it's too frustrating for too many of the students. They're finding the positions too difficult."

It was during this period that I began to hear Martha say things to her Juilliard classes such as "Do you do that in your ballet class? Do you call *that* Fifth Position? How dare you do that in my class? Those legs should be turned-out, not 'sort of'!"

Most dance companies have company classes before their performances. Martha never gave such a class. She believed that all company members should assume the responsibility for doing whatever was necessary to prepare them for performance.

When, however, I began to see company members doing a strict ballet barre before a Graham performance, I questioned strongly how doing a ballet barre would prepare them for the demands of the Graham repertory. There was never a performance in all my years as Martha's leading man, as her partner, before which I did not give myself a full Graham class. And the imagery, all Martha's pieces were flooded with imagery. In order for the dances to evoke their incomparable dramatic power, these images must be there. The teacher and the artistic director should have a responsibility to keep these emotional images and sub-texts alive and glowing.

It is possible, still, that a director will come along, someone who has a thorough knowledge of the works of Martha Graham, who will be uncompromising in seeking the truth of the original artistic impulse from which this marvelous oeuvre emerged. Someone who has the ability to inspire and translate and provide the imagery needed to communicate with generations farther and farther away from the creative wellspring that was Martha Graham.

The passion has to return. The Graham technique is a technique for the theater. Everything has to be motivated from the inner life of the dancer/actor, that is: from the *center*! When this inner life is not involved, sterility sets in. Martha herself has said that "this lack of motivation will lead to meaningless movement, and meaningless movement leads to decadence."

V

To Today

The dancers in this section of the book describe both the continuity and change that characterized the Graham company from the late fifties through her death. Graham retired from performing at age seventy-six, an unusually long career for a dancer, and suffered from depression when she was no longer able to enact her own movement ideas. Clearly, as more members of the company who had knowledge of the dance styles of the thirties, forties, and fifties aged or moved on, Graham needed to develop a teaching syllabus that would enable younger dancers to perpetuate her work.

The ultimate triumph of the Graham company of the seventies and eighties is a testimony to the growth of the school and its many excellent teachers. Through solidifying the syllabus, while still respecting the need for flexibility in approaching dance training, they were able to continue the Graham tradition. The legendary training method could survive even without Graham's performing or daily involvement; this is the promise for the future of Graham teaching.

YURIKO

Yuriko, regisseur of the Martha Graham Dance Company, studied at the University of California, Los Angeles and, although an American citizen, was wrongfully interned in 1942 in a US detention camp. She joined the Martha Graham Dance Company where she stayed from 1944–1967.

From 1944–1967, Yuriko performed on the Broadway stage in roles such as Eliza in Jerome Robbins' stage and screen version of The King and I, *and restaged the same work throughout the US, Israel, London, Tokyo, and for the 1978 Broadway revival. Yuriko has had her own company, taught in many countries, including Poland, Cuba, Costa Rica, and Australia, and received several commissions and an honorary doctorate from France.*

Currently, she is directing the Martha Graham Ensemble, and teaches at the Martha Graham School of Contemporary Dance. In 1989, she assisted Robbins in restaging The King and I *for Jerome Robbins' Broadway.*

I would like to talk about the impression, impact, and logic of the Graham technique.

I arrived in New York in September of 1943 from the Gila River Relocation Center where I was interned by the US government unjustly, with one hundred dollars and a one-way ticket given to me to start anew. I was brave, in a sense, but very, very green. I didn't know New York.

I found a job as a seamstress and in the evenings took classes with Jane Dudley and Sophie Maslow. One evening, in the dressing room, Jane remarked that Martha needed a seamstress. I had a job at the Jay Thorpe department store as a seamstress, but decided to take a leave to sew for Martha as a volunteer. I sewed for *Deaths and Entrances* that premiered in December 1943.

My first impression of the company was a reaction to its power. I saw the work from high up in the balcony looking down on the stage. What I remember of Martha was her fantastic traveling falls across the length of the stage. She came through from one end of the stage to the other in about five falls as I looked on in amazement. I could not imagine how she did that.

Then I remember a dramatic, jerky, sharp movement—how did she do that?

Jane Dudley came across the stage in a swoop of a contraction—a huge wave coming "swoosh"—like that—and into a contraction. "I can't take this anymore," I said to myself.

In late 1944, I became Graham's demonstrator, a position I held for over eight years. It was here that I learned the depth and logic of her teaching. I watched her teach and perform for the next twenty-three years. I learned the dynamics and approach of her basic principle—contraction and release—and witnessed her creativity.

For me, the contraction is an inner action that produces an outer position. The position depends upon how and where you start the contraction. For instance, this explanation of a hanging contraction will illustrate the point.

HANGING CONTRACTION

Kneel on the right knee with the left leg out to the side with a straight knee; the body facing front; and the arms outstretched. Begin a contraction in the left hip moving backwards into the bones of the lower spine in a circular motion—almost a sitting position—and continue the contraction and motion into the right hip. The circular motion then continues as a visualization from the right hip to the right elbow which is held shoulder-high, bent, and with the forearm and hand toward the floor—a right angle of the arm. This position looks as if it were hanging from that elbow.

TRAVELING FALL

The traveling fall that Martha performed so magnificently in *Deaths and Entrances* became part of the technique given in class. This movement begins with a contraction in the right hip, travels through the back bones to create a sitting position, continues through to the left hip where you land in a backfall. The left leg then extends to release the body, contraction is done as it comes around to the front, and a release raises the body to the original position. The movement is then repeated: contraction, a sit, backfall to left side, and a recovery from the kneeling position with an extension of the left leg, a contraction around with the body slightly past the right leg. The movement might be described as a backfall and may be used to travel across the stage when done continuously.

SCULPTURED CONTRACTION

The sculptured contraction is my name for this movement, because when Martha first gave it to us she said that we should feel like a piece of sculpture with holes, such as in a Henry Moore sculpture. That is, we should have the feeling of air going through the holes in our bones. This movement has subsequently changed into a much more sensuous "down" feeling. But here is the original movement: standing on the right leg, knees parallel, lift the left leg into a side *attitude* along the same line as the right supporting leg. The left knee is only slightly bent and the right is in *demi-plié*. A contraction begins on the left side and travels into the back or sit bones with the pelvis parallel to the floor and the contraction ends on the right hip.

The position of the arm: right arm bent and in front of the body. The left arm stretches to the side; the head is turned slightly to the right. Martha said we should visualize air going through holes in our bones and ending in a reach through to the sky from the elbow.

CIRCLE LEG CONTRACTION

This movement begins with a high *rond de jambe* with the right
leg. When the crest of the *rond de jambe* is reached to the side,
a contraction begins in the right hip and moves to the left hip,
almost to a sitting position as the leg continues around to the
back and passes behind the supporting leg that is now in a *demi-
plié* position. The left arm is outstretched as the movement begins
and remains to the side. Both arms finish to the left. The effect
is somewhat like a hovering bird with the torso almost parallel
to the floor at the finish of the movement. The feeling should
be *up* as the leg lifts. Martha described the pelvis as looking up
at the sky as an *under* contraction, and the ending as an *over* contraction.

Because these actions come from the depth of the body as
the source, I believe her technique never goes against the laws
of natural movement in the body.

UPRIGHT STANCE

About forty-five years ago, Martha gave a description of the
stance she wanted us to assume. It is a position I still place myself
into when I rehearse, or teach, for, as she said, "In this properly
balanced position, your body will not become tired."

The stance is maintained in perpendicular lines. Seen from
the side, the ankle bone must be perpendicular to the floor (not
with a pronated arch, but held straight up); the hip bone must
be in a straight line at the natural bend or crease created at the
top of the leg when the leg is raised and the torso kept erect (the
pelvis must not be tipped forward or backward); the shoulder
at the hollow in front and below the clavicle bone should remain
upright (should not drop forward or be held unnaturally back);
the base of the neck should be held in a perpendicular line to
the lobe of the ear; and the forehead between the eyebrows and
hairline should make a straight line.

IMAGES AND EXPRESSIONS

Martha had many images and expressions that helped us visualize the movements. For placement of the face, she would say, "point your ears upward, straight up." In order to have us sense all parts of the body, "Get to know all your pores. Speak to them. Train them until you feel tingles from within. Do not feel flesh hanging on the bone, but a deeper tingling sensation."

Concerning contractions, she suggested we visualize circles spiraling around the outside of our ankles, continuing around and up our legs, hips, waist, chest, head, and up to the sky: "circles within circles within circles . . ."

Concerning falls: "Calculate a danger as if you just tripped and fell."

Concerning contractions: "The contraction comes from the pit of the stomach."

She also illustrated a soundless sound that emanated from the innards to indicate an expression of horror, terror, revulsion, and reaction to base actions, such as the movement of the Chorus in *Night Journey*. Martha described the movement as a "pulling out of the innards from the bowels, a stretching of them to the sky followed by a contraction retracting the innards as if they were on an elastic." This dance depicts a sickness. It's awful.

STUART HODES

Stuart Hodes was a member of the Graham company from 1946–1958, and taught at the Graham school from 1950–1984. He has choreographed for musicals, films, his own concerts, and ballet and modern dance companies.

Hodes has performed in Broadway musicals, on television, and continues to perform, most recently with Steve Koplowitz in a concert at Dance Theatre Workshop. He is on the faculty of Manhattan Community College where he is developing a new dance major program, and is Director of the Dance Notation Bureau. The following is an excerpt from a proposed book by Hodes.

In 1947 Douglas Watson taught me the first piece of Graham choreography I ever learned, the "party step" from *Letter to the World*. It took him two hours to teach me it. That night my metatarsal arch collapsed. I wondered if I was meant to be a dancer.

In 1984, I returned to the Graham school to teach technique. I met Martha after class and mentioned that being there was stimulating.

"How stimulating?" she asked.

"It brings back my early days with you," I said.

She fixed me with a look and said, "Write it down." It surprised me, and I must have shown it. "Stuart, write it down," she said again, commandingly.

Well, I did. Here is a portion about how it was to take Martha's class.

*   *   *   *   *

Martha's advanced class, 1947. The advanced class met at 4:30 PM. By 4:15, the choice spots in the center of the studio floor and in front of the mirrors were taken, and latecomers picked their way to the places near the back and at the sides.

Before starting, I liked to rest in the squatty soles-of-the-feet-together position of the opening moves, letting the weight of my torso gently lengthen the muscles of my lower back. The maple floor, clean as a cutting board, felt good under my bare thighs.

Ethel Winter, the demonstrator, faced the class. Other demonstrators were Yuriko [Kikuchi], Helen McGehee, and Pearl Lang, all members of the Graham Company. One minute before 4:30, Ralph Gilbert entered, sat down at the piano, and arranged his newspaper. When Martha entered, everyone watched her alertly. She looked the class over, glanced toward Ralph, who met her eyes—

"And—!"

Ralph's clean chords cracked out as each torso dropped into opening *bounces*, sixteen with soles of the feet together, sixteen with legs outspread, sixteen extended to the front. *Breathings* followed—an expansion that filled the torso and lifted the gaze. Martha taught it with images, yet the goal was a skill without mystical baggage. In particular, she never allowed breath to whistle in and out yoga-style because the need for breath varied and real breathing had to be free beneath all movement.

Then began those signature torso modulations, Graham *contractions*. From deep in my pelvis I drew my body into a concave arc from hips to head, relishing the sensation of deep muscles working and the surge of force into my bones that seemed to shoot out of my flexed hands and feet. *Release* straightened me like an uncoiling spring.

As each contraction began, my face lifted, lengthening my throat. "Open your eyes!" Martha commanded, and accused us of resistance, self-indulgence, retreat, and other contemptible things if we closed them. "Present your gaze!" she exhorted, and I presented mine to the vaulted ceiling, then through it imagining sky, space, and beyond space. My gaze felt solid, as though it had weight. I panned it like a beam and chopped it down like a cleaver as my body gathered an accelerating sweep that articulated my spine and flowed through my torso into my mouth where it burst into a second contraction to begin again.

"Sit to the side, Fourth Position."

Ethel Winter demonstrated and I studied her closely, trying to fathom the comfort and ease she had in this curious body posture. My tendons seemed long enough, but I was never at home in the sitting-Fourth Position and believed it to be a flaw of understanding, some muscle group deep inside that hadn't learned not to resist.

The sitting Fourth generates a spiral in the body. A year earlier Martha had urged us to see the French film *Farrabique*, a story of birth and death on a French family farm. She particularly wanted us to notice the stop-motion sequences of plants growing. "Watch how they spiral upward toward the sun," she said. "Life flows along a spiral path." Soon I noticed that spirals were being emphasized in many of our technical moves and introduced into others. Decades later the scientists Crick and Watson discovered that the DNA molecule is one spiral within another. Martha's intuition was scientifically confirmed.

I extended my legs, tilted onto my right side, spread my knees, and pulled back onto the left rump, each move on a percussive chord. Ralph's music was familiar, yet his improvisation was always fresh. Once into the exercise, an elusive melody in a minor key appeared, inspired perhaps by the subtle coil of the hips.

My left hip lifted to insinuate a rotating wave through my stomach, chest, and head. My arms engaged, first left, then right, then both as head and gaze swept an arc. The room spun past my eyes yet left stillness within me. Both hips rose as my torso arched up, back, and around until my weight hung suspended over my right forearm where I floated until a contraction caught me, sucked me up and whirled me into a ball, until release opened me up again to end the move with a delicate flicker—like silk settling.

End of the set. Suspended in the stillness that followed deep effort, I relished my quickened heartbeat and presented my gaze to the mirror where thirty others presented their gazes to me.

Martha moved about giving corrections. She stopped over me. "Go to the count of five." I spiraled back, placing weight on my right forearm. She poked me lightly under the ribs. "Lift, *there*." I strove into my rib cage. "At lease you're wet," she said. It was approval. The floor was wet too as sweat ran off my thighs and arms. Heavy sweating felt cleansing—a shower from the inside out. The room was hot, comforting the muscles, the air nourishing as broth.

"Over on your face." I stretched out face down, body parallel to the front wall. "Back on your knees. Exercise-on-six." Martha's most dramatic floor sequence was named simply by the number of its counts.

I came to the starting position: body shaped like a "Z"; weight on knees and insteps; torso thrust out horizontally from the hips. Martha looked us over. "Lengthen your torso. Keep your back parallel to the floor, like a table."

She pushed gently on the hips of the dancer beside me to lower her torso, lifted another's shoulders, traced her finger along the spine of one who wasn't in a full release, pressed down a pair of tensely lifted heels. She took her time. Simply holding the position demanded strength so Martha kept us there. I wished she would start, not quite comfortable with my weight on my knees, or rather on the tops of my tibia just below the kneecaps. I felt my jaw tighten and consciously relaxed it, then tried to let go with every muscle not engaged by the position.

"One!" A powerful contraction lifted the center of my back as my head and shoulders scooped toward the floor. My torso lifted and unfolded moving into a steep backward tilt from knees to head.

"Two!" The count caught the tilt and I held it, thighs lengthened from within. (Years later, a student from Japan, Akiko Kanda, transformed herself with the exercise-on-six. She'd arrived with muscle-heavy thighs giving her slender torso a grounded look. But she took class three times a day and did the exercise-on-six with fierce intensity. In a year her thighs were like reeds. She became a leading dancer in the Graham Company and no one could believe she'd ever been other than the steely sylph who appeared onstage.)

"Three!" I sprang into release, the body-long contraction reversed in one count.

"Four!" The release sucked back into a second contraction and steeper tilt, buttocks inches from heels, at the limit of my strength for half a count—

"And—release, sit," buttocks dropped onto heels, head back, gaze straight up, spine striving for length as the torso continued forward toward the floor, in "hyper-release."

"Five—" the release folded into a contraction.

"And—six!" to the horizontal thrust of the opening position.

We started over. Exercise-on-six was always performed at least twice.

"Sit to the side." I settled gratefully off my knees. Martha nodded to Ethel. Ethel had done everything along with us but now she did the exercise-on-six by herself—slowly—as Martha explained the impulse beneath each move. Ethel did it effortlessly, her control almost casual in positions that had made my muscles shudder.

All dance classes had demonstrators because dance is best learned directly from one body to another. Demonstrators faced the class, danced every exercise as our mirror image, and repeated moves as many times as the teacher asked. Being Martha's demonstrator was a high honor and as tough as boot camp. Then it was our turn and we did the exercise-on-six four times more. It yielded, at last, a feeling of exultation.

"Rise from the floor." We stretched out at full length on our stomachs then pushed back onto hands and knees.

"One!" The leg reached back.

"Two!" Step onto the left leg, straighten the right, line up heel-hip-head.

"Three!" Rise on the left leg as the body turns toward the mirror and the right leg scissors in, coming to meet the left in First Position.

Mini-break—fifteen seconds. (Men tuck T-shirts into trunks and subtly adjust dance belts. Women pull leotard bottoms over exposed buttocks.)

"Brushes."

We began with the legs parallel, weight on one, the other beating like a bird's wing. "Make arrows!" said Martha, behind me.

I thought of a man who had come to class a month before, placing himself in the front row. He wasn't a bad dancer except for having unfortunate feet that were large, lumpy, and made slapping noises against the floor. It disturbed Martha but he seemed blithely unaware and bounded enthusiastically through the class with a happy smile. Martha had interrupted our last leaps across the floor and sent the whole class to the barre for a series of foot exercises. She ended the class with these words. "These are exercises you can do at home. I want you to do them every day. And one year from now you will return with feet like arrows . . . not hot-water bottles!"

That was in my mind as I strove to point my feet on each brush. The brushes broke free of the floor and then pulsed higher, coming parallel to the horizon at a tempo faster than the internal pendulum rhythm so that the body had to absorb the effort, or reveal it. Martha was still behind me.

"You're gripping with your arms. Let go. Let light pass through your body." I responded with a shake of my torso as I tried to disconnect my arms from the force energizing my leg. At the same time, I used the image she gave me, trying to feel transparent, trying to float serenely above the commotion of my legs below. I tried to imagine that my pumping leg was entirely separate from me, with a job to do: I encouraged it in a friendly, yet impersonal, way.

We did deep *pliés*, joining every dancer who ever lived. My body neared the floor, knee-angle acute as the bones lost mechanical advantage, straining thigh muscles that had to support me with sheer strength. "Lift!" exhorted Martha and I tried to imagine gravity flowing upward through my body, opposite to jumps where the thrust is down; resolution was often sought in opposites. I believed that, with enough concentration, opposition could disappear and effort with it.

"Slow sits to the floor!"

We began in a wide Second Position, spilled weight onto the left leg, body curved like a taut sail, right foot passing behind and to the left of the left foot, sickling at the ankle—a sin in ballet but with a beauty of its own. My instep caressed the floor and accepted my weight until my right buttock touched the floor. I settled into the sit. Thirty dancers held it, dynamic, curve-powered coils of muscle from knee to shoulder.

Ralph turned the page of his newspaper while he held the pedal down. His ringing chord echoed the effort as Martha counted ". . . six, seven, eight," and Ralph slammed his forearm down on fifteen keys at once. Thirty backs snapped straight flinging weight through thighs and sickled feet into skin-polished floor. Thirty torsos cut upward to a high suspension, then settled carefully, like mountain birds landing. The music drained away.

Martha had Ethel demonstrate prances, then challenged us with a look that seemed to ask "Why don't you all dance like that?" The first time I saw Ethel dance, she was as chaste as Diana the Huntress in a *Letter to the World* rehearsal. Next it was jazz improvisations at a company party, and after that steamy routines in Broadway's *Texas, L'il Darlin'*.

Daydreaming, I missed an explanation. I suddenly felt woozy and bent from the waist to drain blood into my brain, then did the prances as a rest step, letting the spring in my calves and feet carry me through the first low set. We repeated it knees rising high, then with jumps in the middle, ending with a double upbeat. Martha worked the prances into a turning jump combination with tricky syncopation, and I attacked it with gusto forgetting to be tired.

A second mini-break while the class shuffled to the corner and lined up in pairs for the diagonal across the floor. Men always danced last. There were only three other men, Mark Ryder (whom we called Sasha) and Robert Cohan, both in the Graham company, and a smallish wiry newcomer in a white leotard whose horn-rimmed glasses were tied on with elastic. Cohan and the newcomer hung back wanting to go last so I paired up with Sasha.

We began with low walks, slowly at first, then faster, trying to keep the body centered between footfalls. After several crosses, Martha gave a ludicrous illustration, chest caved in, belly thrust out, chin poked forward. "Little babies walk like that. Selfish little babies." Her quick smile didn't fool anybody. She hated what we were doing. We started again.

"No!" She stopped us. "Watch Ethel."

Ethel moved in a seamless flow, knees flexing smoothly, toes touching the floor with the delicacy of fingers, inviting the heel that followed soundlessly with her weight—around the room, gliding like on tracks. "Do it!" We did it over and over, fast, then faster, developing into low runs that swallowed the studio in three seconds.

"Triplets." One low step, two high. Martha added a wide turn, a traveling skip, and worked up a dancy combination that reversed and cut back in a semi-circle with leaps the length of the studio. Ralph hammered out the triplets on low notes, then put a four-beat under the leaps with a slashing chord accented on the second beat to give us a musical lift at the crest of the jump.

"Stop!" Martha clapped her hands together halting music and dancers. "You're missing it," she said angrily. "Push off on one, stay in the air on two. Listen to Ralph. He's trying his best to help you. Sasha and Stuart, will you please demonstrate?"

A bouquet! We leaped in unison trying to out jump each other, aware of the intermediate students watching from the doorway as they waited for their class to begin. Then everyone did leaps in a sustained crescendo until the clock said three minutes after six.

"We've run over. That's all. Thank you."

Intermediate students dashed into the studio while the advanced class applauded.

DAVID WOOD

David Wood, a member of the Graham company from 1953–1967, acted as rehearsal director for the company as well. Wood began his career as a performer in Broadway musicals, the New York City Opera, and Metropolitan Opera companies. He also appeared with Hanya Holm, Doris Humphrey, José Limón, Charles Weidman, and Alwin Nikolais.

Wood has taught for Holm and Weidman, at the American Dance Festival at Connecticut College, the High School for the Performing Arts in New York City, as well as in Sweden, Mexico, Vera Cruz, Béjart's Mudra school in Brussels, Jerusalem, Japan, and Norway. As a choreographer, Wood has created works for summer stock, musicals, his own company, a PBS program, and has been the recipient of NEA Fellowships in 1973 and 1979.

Currently, Wood has created a dance major program at the University of California at Berkeley, and the Bay Area Repertory Dance Company, a performing off-shoot of the program. In 1987, Wood received the Distinguished Teacher Award from the University of California at Berkeley.

The technique, the performance, and the choreography of Martha Graham are closely interwoven. The only time I ever heard Martha speak of choreographing for men was at a press conference when she said, "I'm not a man, I've never been a man, and I have no intention of ever being a man. I first suggest, and then I alter, change, and shape the movement that occurs in order to arrive at male choreography."

An example of how this happened is when Martha choreographed the Messenger of Death on me in *Clytemnestra* (1958).
She spent a month developing the concept and then gave me
a pole, a musician, and sent me upstairs to work on the movement by myself. After two days, I presented her with what I
thought was a marvelous finished product. She looked at it,
sighed and began to cut, change, suggest, add, and demand what
she wanted. My movement was merely a catalyst that set off her
imagination. What she created was totally her own product.

When I first learned the technique, it was said that it was
not really good for men. The reason given was that a woman
had created it. This made as much sense to me as a statement
that ballet should only be done by males, because Louis XIV was
one of the first performers and protagonists of this art form.

The fact that Graham's work was at first done by women
was a factor in this statement. But it did not take into account
that the floorwork, in particular, challenged the male dancer and
was extremely beneficial in expanding the range of motion in
the pelvic area while, at the same time, teaching many different
qualities of movement.

With the advent of males as members of the company, the
technique broadened in scope, but did not basically change. Erick
Hawkins' appearance in *American Document* (1938) added weight
and strength to the movement it had not had before. Then Merce
Cunningham in *Every Soul Is a Circus* (1939), *Letter to the World*
(1940), and *El Penitente* (1940) added another dimension in elevation and utilized a certain square approach to movement for
men that Martha developed at that time.

Letter to the World used the first male group in a Graham
work, but Martha did not greatly alter or make changes to her
technique for the sake of male movement. Within some variation, the party scene—the main dance for both males and
females—kept the relationship of the sexes, but more by the relationship itself than by the movement.

In *Deaths and Entrances* (1943), the male became more con-
ceptual, with the mens' dance and the fight between the Poetic
Beloved and the Dark Beloved characters. In *Dark Meadow* (1946),
in the "Sarabande," the men began to support the women, and
the very first lifts—simple but beautiful—were done. In the "Fet-
ish Dance," the man became a distinct sexual being.

In *Diversion of Angels* (1948), Martha choreographed two distinct male and female groups. Within one context of lyrical young love, the men and women moved clearly and distinctly in their own worlds using their own particular unique strengths. Now and then, the two groups merged their energies to become unified. The sexuality of the White, Red, and Yellow Couples was more clearly discernible against the background of group conformity. I always felt the group movement itself could easily be reversed, because it fit structurally both the male and female bodies. But, here again, the intent was made clear within the sexual relationship rather than the movement.

Phaedra (1962) showed the peak development during this period of male athleticism with the creation of the Bull Dancers. The mens' entrance with the leap and sit to the floor actually ended with one man diving into the thighs of the other. This sheer physical exuberance opened the door for later acrobatics and athleticism. However, at a later point, when I saw the company on tour, half of the men were replaced by women in this dance which was an historically accurate thing to do. The women did the movements successfully.

With the arrival of males in the company, there came some new movements: In *Diversion of Angels*, the Bisons that cut into the air (however, these movements were also performed very fast, dartingly, and brilliantly by Helen McGehee); in *Letter to the World* (1940), the march jumps were introduced by Merce Cunningham (however, in *Night Journey* [1947], the womens' contraction jumps were basically the same, only more difficult and more powerful); the contraction leaps are brilliantly performed by men (but consider the weighted leaps in *Primitive Mysteries* [1931], done by the women—they are powerful and beautiful); in the beginning of *Ardent Song* (1954), the curtain rose with the men on one side and the women on the other side of Yuriko as both groups began the same movement (in the rest of the dance, male and female groups developed separately, but in the beginning, the two sections were one and split apart only later).

The main change brought about by the introduction of male athleticism was the expansion of the movement vocabulary. The inner landscape expanded as the cyclical action began to include the outer landscape. There were never any absolute limits as to which movements were male and which were female except in class. There, a differentiation was made for the movement, because a slow pace was given hopefully for the achievement of higher elevation by the men. In class, there was always some interchange of quality rather than a development of sexual stereotypes. Robert Powell's extensions were the envy of many a woman; Dudley Williams' fast lightness; and Bob Cohan's beautiful lyricism were in evidence.

On the other hand, who could fail to remember the marvelous female power of Pearl Lang as the Seductress Death in *Canticle for Innocent Comedians* (1952), or even more so, all the power of Martha in so many roles, but especially as she did the knee crawls along the red cloth enticing Agamemnon to his death in *Clytemnestra* (1958).

Male athleticism did affect the expansion and the explosive strength of the technique. But the marvel was that there were no limits placed upon an individual because of his or her sex, but rather the focal point was on the unique projection of the individual as a human being. This development then proceeded to the ultimate, powerful use of the individual by Martha as male or female in its dimension to create her later choreographic complexities.

TAKAKO ASAKAWA

Takako Asakawa was born in Tokyo, Japan and joined the Graham company in 1962 where she remains a principal dancer today.

She came to the United States in 1960, after studying in Tokyo, with the show Holiday in Japan. *She is married to David Hatch Walker with whom she formed the Asakawalker Company to create works in recital.*

I first came to the technique in 1962, and because Martha's background was in Denishawn and Oriental dance, I found it quite easy for me to understand because my background is Oriental.

There is a use of the ground—the pull of gravity—and the use of the upper back, as well as the yoga connection—breathing—that made the technique easy for me.

Technique is important, but soul is more important. You have to project what you feel. If that is not there, the technique is empty and does not really matter. So I would say that while Martha had physical gifts, and developed her technique, she also developed her soul. And that was more important.

PETER SPARLING

Peter Sparling danced with the Martha Graham Dance Company from 1973–1987. He is a native of Michigan where he attended Interlochen Arts Academy. At the Juilliard School, he was awarded the Louis Horst Memorial Scholarship and became a member of the José Limón Dance Company.

Sparling presented his dance company in 1983 for five successive seasons. He has taught and choreographed at the Juilliard School, Australia's Victoria College of the Arts, Portugal's Ballet Gulbenkian, ABT II, Taiwan's Cloudgate Contemporary Dance Theatre, the London Contemporary Dance Theatre, and the Laban Bartenieff Institute of Movement Studies.

Currently, Sparling is assistant professor of dance at the University of Michigan in Ann Arbor.

Those of us who came into the company in the 1970s followed in the footsteps of so many wonderful dancers. We had the Rosetta Stone—the technique—a presence unto itself. We had role models, the dancers we had seen on stage. Although we were coming into a company quite green—the apprentice company became the main company in 1973—we held onto the technique. But times had changed.

We learned the roles in the apprenticeship company under the direction of Bertram Ross and Mary Hinkson, or in Juilliard, but we were children of the media and with the proliferation of dance at that time, it was important for us to fill a Broadway house during a season.

The pressure was on. We had spent many weeks learning the roles and handling the props; learning from films; and although the choreography was learned, it was up to us to bring the roles to life, as they had been done in the previous decades. We were not involved in the creation of the dances, although Martha was always creating, but we knew we would be compared to members of the original casts.

Many times, the critics and the public labeled us light-weight, without the maturity or the gravity of dancers in past Graham companies. That taught us all a lesson. We had to go back continually to Martha's original ideas, as they were embedded in the technique, to get deeper into the roles that we saw in videocassette or film versions. The actual strength of a live performance was not there for us to see. And the mechanics of running the video machine was intrusive and disruptive: rewind, press, pause.

We are now taking the repertoire into an era of long touring, annual seasons, and five performances a week. The technique was what we depended upon, not only to maintain our stamina and to keep our roots, but to give us the source and motivation for the emotional content.

I think we can see today how Martha's idiosyncratic gifts influenced the technique and how the artistic goals contributed to the technique as well. The progression is marvelous to observe over the years—how it all developed into a streamlined and expanded form.

For me, it is proof of the strength of that technique that I can go on my way and be as idiosyncratic as I want to be, and still depend upon the basic structure and principles of the Graham technique.

Martha was the first to say that she stole from the best and that she expected us to do the same. I've taken her at her word. We have not only learned from her a physical way to move, but we've learned an attitude toward life, toward theater, and a moral obligation to an audience to find and project something significant.

CHRISTINE DAKIN

Christine Dakin has been a member of the Martha Graham Dance Company since 1976. She studied and performed in the companies of Pearl Lang and Kazuko Hirabayashi as well.

Dakin is a member of the faculty at the Martha Graham School of Contemporary Dance in New York City. She has been a guest artist-teacher at the University of Michigan, Duke University, the University of Guanajuato in Mexico, and at the Lincoln Center Institute.

Q. What do you think about the fact that so many former Graham dancers have said that the entire movement system is no longer taught?

Dakin: I'm not sure why that is true, but I don't think it's a question of right or wrong, or its being bad or good. Change in dance and in a technique is natural. Martha herself was constantly in the process of change and growth, and that is reflected in which parts of the technique are taught and how the movement develops. It may be that teachers who have not experienced the older parts of the technique feel uncomfortable in teaching it, and that today's students are not comfortable with the physical demands of the older technique.

For the most part, all the movement that forms the historical parts of the technique are in Martha's choreography. In reality, not many of the students are going to be involved in learning the choreography, performing in the company, so it has some validity to concentrate the teaching on a more general body of exercises supplemented with repertory workshops and special courses.

Q. Which movements in the syllabus system seem to be missing?

Dakin: It's hard to say, because the technique is not a finite or static entity. Dancers are always remembering and forgetting exercises as they teach, and drawing from the new choreography for new material. You have to keep in mind that Martha created choreography, not exercises, so the shape classroom exercises take is somewhat up to the teacher.

Dancers today want an exact description of exercises, when in reality they are phrases of dances that may have no specific answer; is it turned-in or turned-out? It can't always be broken down.

From my experience with old films, and working with the previous generation of teachers, I can say that a body of the floorwork is missing. These were part of the germinating process of Martha's work, worked out on her own and her dancers' bodies at that time, and reflect a very different kind of body and physicality. It is quite beautiful to see and it would be good to try and retrieve some of it, but the basic principles are still embodied in the core of the exercises today.

Q. Is there actually a syllabus?

Dakin: Yes, the faculty has a syllabus it works from. Obviously it is different from earlier syllabi as it contains some of the more recent additions to the technique and leaves out some others. The choreography has given us a vocabulary of movement that is vast and can be taught as a series that progresses from exercises that work for beginners to their more complex developments for advanced students.

Q. If the entire technique is not taught, how do people who are taken into the company learn these movements in order to perform the dances as created by the choreographer?

Dakin: You learn these things as they come. The basics are taught to everyone and you learn to apply those basics to new situations. The rehearsal directors and the other dancers help, and you learn the movements as Martha created them, within a dramatic context of the individual dance, which helps tremendously.

Q. What is the requirement for a student who wants to study dance?

Martha Graham in *Scène Javanaise*, 1926. Photograph by Nickolas Muray, courtesy The Dance Collection, New York Public Library, Astor, Lenox, and Tilden Foundations.

Primitive Mysteries, c. 1931. Back row: Gertrude Shurr, Marie Marchowsky, unidentified. Middle: Martha Graham. Front row: Anna Sokolow, Anita Alvarez, unidentified. Photograph by Soichi Sunami, courtesy Gertrude Shurr.

Primitive Mysteries, c. 1931. Sophie Maslow, Martha Graham. Photographer unknown, courtesy Sophie Maslow.

Anna Sokolow and Anita Alvarez, unidentified dance, c. 1931.
Photographer unknown, courtesy Anna Sokolow.

Martha Graham leads a technique class at the Connecticut College
American Dance Festival, c. 1960. Photograph © Terry Estate, courtesy
The Dance Collection, New York Public Library.

Letter to the World, 1940. Martha Graham and Jean Erdman. Photograph © Barbara Morgan, courtesy Jean Erdman and Lloyd Morgan.

Letter to the World, c. 1940. Martha Graham, Jane Dudley, Sophie Maslow. Photographer unknown, courtesy Sophie Maslow.

Martha Graham and John Butler at the Connecticut College American
Dance Festival, c. 1940s. Photographer unknown, courtesy John Butler.

Deaths and Entrances, 1943. Erick Hawkins, Martha Graham, John Butler.
Photograph © Cris Alexander, courtesy John Butler.

Appalachian Spring, 1944. Clockwise from top: Merce Cunningham, May O'Donnell, Erick Hawkins, Martha Graham. Photograph © Cris Alexander, courtesy May O'Donnell.

Acrobats of God, 1957. David Wood. Photograph by Martha Swope, courtesy David Wood.

Martha Graham leading a rehearsal for *Episodes* in 1959. Middle row: Helen McGehee, Linda Hodes, and Akiko Kanda. Back row: Bill Carter, Kenneth Peterson, Bertram Ross, and Paul Nickel. Photographer unknown, courtesy *Dance Magazine*.

Clytemnestra, revival, 1966. Helen McGehee. Photographer unknown, courtesy Helen McGehee.

Embattled Garden, revival. Yuriko. Date and photographer unknown, courtesy Yuriko.

Seraphic Dialogue, revival, 1986. Christine Dakin. Photograph by Martha Swope, courtesy Christine Dakin.

Peter Sparling in an unidentified dance. Photograph by Frank Richards, courtesy Peter Sparling.

Dakin: As with any kind of movement, dance requires first a desire to move, to explore oneself moving. For Martha's technique in particular, there must be a willingness to push the limits we believe we have, to enter into each class as a new challenge, a ritual which leads us to deepen our awareness, concentrate our energies, expand our ability.

Q. Is ballet a larger influence now than it was earlier?

Dakin: I think dancers of necessity have had to become more versatile to meet today's expectations. Martha was much more interested in using movement that came directly from ballet in her later works than she previously was, and it both changed and broadened her movement vocabulary. Naturally, as always, we dancers had to keep up with her.

Q. How long does it take to master today's syllabus?

Dakin: As you know, on the deepest level, it is a life's work. On a more practical level, we have four levels of classes and a certification program that takes about three years to complete. It consists of as much technique as possible, music, composition, repertory classes, teaching seminars, and performances.

Inevitably, dancers want to teach what they have been taught. Good dancers don't necessarily make good teachers.

Q. Is there a procedure or a mechanism in place that assures correct teaching of the movements?

Dakin: This is the reason for the certification course. It does assure that the minimum understanding of the technique has been achieved. The rest is a matter of individual ability, of course. I think, as a general rule, someone who has been with the company is a better choice of teacher, because in performing the choreography you can discover *why* you are doing what you do in the classroom. Your goal as a teacher is clearer as you see the breadth of Martha's dramatic world, and the physical means it requires to express it.

Q. What is the goal?

Dakin: The goal is to pass on the technique Martha created, but not as so many steps or exercises. Nothing could be further from her concept of dance. She drew movement out of herself to portray characters and emotions. It is pieces of this dance that we call exercises. In recreating that movement for ourselves, we must turn it back into dance, and hope to find a glimpse of the core from which it came.

Q. Are the students chosen on a scholarship basis?

Dakin: Our school is open to anyone. Few nongovernment sponsored schools can choose only the most talented students. I have seen Martha, however, come into a class and threaten to kick them all out of her school. The class shapes up very quickly after that. It was her way of demanding the concentration and work required to master her technique.

Q. How do you see modern dance changing during your career?

Dakin: I see all of dance moving in the direction of athleticism and tricks. Audiences are easily entertained by this, but it dulls them, I think, to more subtle parts of choreography. Especially for Martha's work, the technique shouldn't be noticed for itself, since it is the means to show the soul of a character. On the other had, Martha's technique has always been a bravura technique, starting with her own incredible body and the extraordinary things she did to create larger-than-life characters, and universal ideas. As audiences get less opportunities to see subtlety, the excitement of stillness, the control of raw energy, and above all a theatricality, Martha's work is increasingly unique. She didn't want to entertain, or have you like it, just be touched, aroused by what she did. We as Graham dancers are also very fortunate to have so many dancers who came before to pass down the choreography and teaching. It gives us a continuity that is powerful, and increases our responsibility to maintain the integrity of the work. It is deeply satisfying to learn Martha's dances from those who did it before, then to enjoy it as your own.

Q. When does all this commitment begin?

Dakin: It can be as young as a child or a teenager. Many people studied with Martha for a good part of their lives. She always enjoyed the energy and creativity of children, though the more visceral aspects of the technique are hard to pass on at that stage. The teenagers are self-conscious and just becoming aware of their own physicality. It is an interesting time to see them make discoveries through the technique.

Q. How would you sum up what has been said about Graham movement by the performers of the past and present?

Dakin: Everyone seems to share a joy in the physical experience of the technique, and in having found such a profound way to express oneself through movement. Martha's theater, her dance, is really a ritual on many levels, one we all share in some way, and which we carry within us always.

PART TWO

Syllabus of Graham Movements

The Martha Graham School

The Martha Graham School of Contemporary Dance is housed in a three-story, red-brick building at 316 East 63rd Street in New York City. The building has been the home of the school since 1952 when it was donated by Lila Acheson Wallace, a patron of the arts. It dates from the turn of the century and was the home of several organizations, including a dance school and a training school for show dogs, before it was purchased for Graham. The Graham school, apprentice company, and the administration of the company are all housed in it.

Here, Graham taught her "acrobats of God," rehearsed her company, and created her dances. More than 400 students practice in the small studio to the left of the hallway, or in the large studio past the narrow admissions desk. Off the hallway is a tiny room—supposedly Graham's private office—although it is always filled with dancers viewing videotapes of Graham's works, overflowing with music scores, practice props, bits of costume, and visitors who come to have a "private" chat about the workings of the school or the company. Upstairs, the administration offices squeeze into cubicles that resemble rooms in an attic, although a more modern office is also maintained in another building.

When a red ribbon was tied to the doors of the large studio on the first floor, everyone knew that a rehearsal was in progress conducted by Graham herself. Graham, a small figure, would be seated and centered in front of the mirrored wall, most often in a smart and simple black or purple Oriental-styled outfit with long pants and sleeves. Her hair was always drawn back from her chiseled features; soft slippers were on her feet. She would often tuck her arthritic hands into the sleeves of her blouse, especially if photos were being taken of her. But her husky voice remained unmuted, and her manner of speaking was half-childish and half-oracular.

It was in studios such as these on 63rd Street that Graham created her dances, taught, and developed the style of costume and makeup that is recognized throughout the world as her own. Graham regarded herself as a performer, not a choreographer. She never warmed-up at the theater; she performed her warm-ups in her hotel room on tour or in early morning Pilates-based sessions at Robert Fitzgerald's studio when she was in New York. Her technique was prodigious and her body natural for dance; her dramatic talent legendary. Gravity, which she treated with such respect and reverence, overtook her body at the age of seventy-six and she stopped performing. "My body will no longer do what I want it to do," she admitted.

Graham made these comments about her training regimen to me in an interview conducted for a radio program in 1963. "I'm fortunate to have a building for a school. It's a darling little building. The dancers are not supposed to run around the garden or the school in bare feet. I scold them for it. They must dance in bare feet in the studio because that's part of their costume, and they must come to class with beautifully clean feet and organized bodies ready for work.

"The school is a disciplined place because there is only one freedom. And that freedom is discipline. I think the only freedom we have in life is what we choose and select to discipline ourselves about. When people are not willing to do that, they have no freedom. Freedom is discipline. It is a philosophy for all of life whether your discipline is law or language. If you have not disciplined yourself in what you choose, then you do not have the courage to break its laws. It is the people who have broken the old laws that have become great figures.

"I prefer to have my students begin to study dance at the age of nine, and I don't object to previous training. I would prefer that it be in ballet for the simple reason that Western dance stems out of more than 300 years of study. There are certain things that one has to learn: the five positions, for instance. These positions are in every dance in the world, even in Indonesian and Cambodian dance, where the Fifth Position has been in Asia for hundreds and hundreds of years. The use of the *plié* and the use of the body is different, but any discipline that is not imposed emotionally or by fantasy on the body, and is not rigid in the sense that it is against the body, is wonderful to begin with. My only fear is always with people who decide they want to begin with what I would call 'creativity'—and I use that word in the sense of just letting oneself go—instead of permitting themselves to go away from tradition after having a thorough knowledge of what one is going away from.

"A musician, for instance, learns certain marvelous rules and abides by them. But when a *great* composer decides to break those rules, it is not because he does not know them, but because he does know.

"The demands of our century require that another dimension to movement, another accepted use of the language of the body, be made. An artist is not ahead of his time; an artist is of his time. Movement is very different from what it used to be in our society and in other places as well. I received a clipping from an Indonesian paper just this last week from a dancer who studied with me. Her audience was deeply disturbed, in a way, by a performance of her dancers, but they still thought it was absolutely marvelous, as well. The girls were dressed in tights and leotards, and were extending the legs higher than the hips, where in their dance, a leg is never extended very much higher than the floor. You see, it all has to do with freedom of the spirit. What moves the spirit in its time makes the outer changes that we see in dance."

THE SYLLABUS

This syllabus lists basic exercises with their variations that indicate advancing levels of accomplishment. The syllabus may or may not be taught in its entirety depending upon the decision of the school or the teacher. The number of executions of each exercise, as well, is an individual choice of the teacher. But the sequence of movements—floorwork, breathings, knees, standing center work, barre, and traveling across the floor—are usually taught in order.

The quotations are from Graham; she frequently described movements using balletic terms. The contraction and release principle is used throughout the classwork and in almost all exercises. As with all physical activity, none of the movements should be attempted without proper instruction.

FLOORWORK

1. Bounces executed in a sitting position
   a. In contraction and release, with feet arched, heels off the ground, toes together, knees and thighs lifted
   b. With legs opened into Second Position
   c. With legs together straight front, feet flexed

   The back ("tree of life") is kept straight from the bottom of the spine to the top of the head as the student sits on the floor. After each bounce, the body is centered. It should feel lifted or suspended "as though you were jumping in the air." The arms are to the side on the floor.

2. Breathings
   a. From contraction to release
   b. Lifting the head

   The throat is felt to be "open" and is centered exactly over the body. The chin is raised when the head is lifted, which permits the head to roll backwards without compressing the neck.

   c. Into a spiral with head

   A spiral is a twist from the waist. It should feel as if "an arrow were going through the body from underneath the shoulders to the hip bones." At all times, the dancer should feel "poised, as if in flight," when seated.

    d.   With an extension to Second Position and a quarter turn on the floor

Variation: with centered contraction to back and a quarter turn onto one hip.

  3. Soles of the feet together (heels up)
      a.   Contract and release
      b.   Contract and release with body forward
      c.   Repeat with the legs open in Second Position

Exercises 1–3 finish with a high lift of the back, chest, and head. Arms open from overhead into Second Position. The lignment of the body in Second Position when it bounces forward is described as "parallel to the ceiling and to the floor." The arms "are like wings" when they open to Second Position. The Second Position on the floor "is not a position of rest, but a position of activity." The muscles of the inside of the leg must be firmly held in order not to deform the outside of the leg from overuse.

  4. Stretches on four counts forward
      a.   With arms in Second Position
      b.   With fingers touching overhead, arms in a diamond shape
      c.   With arms diagonally up
      d.   With soles of the feet together (as in exercise 1a., feet arched and heels up) and hands on ankles
  5. Feet coming forward (straightening front toward the mirror or front of the room)
      a.   With flex and point in the last position (4d.)
      b.   Flex and point with legs straight
      c.   Contract and release with feet pointing and flexing in a drawn-up (knees slightly bent) First Position of the feet

Variation: with extension of one leg extended off the floor front and to the side. The leg is lifted about 45 degrees off the floor and placed back into position, not dropped.

  6. Legs in Second Position
      a.   With one knee slightly bent, flex the foot; straighten the knee, extend the leg, and point the foot

b.   With arms together in front (waist high), or one forward, the other to the side

c.   With spiral in the body. "The body turns only as far as it can with both hips on the floor."

d.   With arms lifted to center overhead (diamond shape)

Variation: with contraction and release. The variation finds the release in a spiral position with one arm raised, the other to the side. "In the contraction to the side, the shoulder crosses the knee."

7. Sitting in Fourth Position

The Fourth Position on the floor begins with the front leg, knee up and the foot on the floor. The back leg's inner thigh is on the floor as the starting position. The front knee is dropped to the floor, outer thigh muscles flat when the exercise begins. The body leans slightly backwards and forwards during this exercise. "This series is only possible when the elemental has been mastered."

a.   Spirals with slight lean backwards

b.   Using one arm

c.   Using two arms

d.   Spiral onto the elbow with contraction and release to the front

Variation: with rise to the knee. "This movement depends not only upon the balance of the body, but on the demonic—fierce—use of the thigh muscles. There is no strain on the knee." The movement of the spiral impels the body onto the back knee in a kneeling position. "There are no exercises for the knees. Only for the muscles surrounding the knees."

Variation: with quarter turns on the contraction. In this quarter turn, the body slides along the floor in the contraction.

8. Back extensions in Fourth Position

The back leg lifts off the floor to its natural capacity. "The hip, thigh, knee, and foot are lifted as the body turns in the spiral variation in the opposite direction from the lifted leg. The heel of the front leg is kept directly in front of the body in relationship to the navel."

a.   Plain, or extended along the floor, hands on floor

b.   With arm extended front

    c.   With quarter turn (a pivot on the front hip that turns the body) along the floor

    d.   With double contraction

9. Front and back extensions

The front extension finds the forward knee extended along the floor at first, and then raised slightly off the floor.

    a.   Plain (along the floor, not lifted)

    b.   With contraction along the floor

    c.   With a high release and rise onto front knee in a quarter turn

    d.   The same as 9c., with a half turn

10. Contraction prone ("This exercise is sometimes called 'pleading.'")

"As in all the exercises, the timing must be correct" to provide the proper shape and execution of the movement.

    a.   Head back on the rise and release

    b.   With head roll forward

    c.   With a half turn and release (pivot on the floor)

    d.   With one leg extended as the body comes up

    e.   With a turn as the leg is extended

11. Sitting in Fourth Position

    a.   Extension of front foot to Second Position off the floor

    b.   With a quarter turn (pivot on floor as leg opens)

    c.   Extension of back leg off the floor with rise onto front knee and continuing to bring the back leg to the Second Position and front as in *rond de jambe*; the foot is placed over the front knee at the end and the sitting position is resumed

12. Contractions around the leg (a difficult and quickly paced series)

    a.   Contraction around the raised knee (as in 11c.)

    b.   With head dropping to place the ear to the ankle; "the head must drop as close to the floor as possible"

    c.   With arms around the raised knee

    d.   With arms (side, overhead, diagonal)

    e.   With backfall in contraction (leaning slightly to the side opposite the raised knee, arms reaching forward)

Variation: with arms and fall (arms overhead).

13. Variations on the above with a spiral; various arm positions; extending front leg on the release. "The strength of one's back, not an arbitrary level, determines the height of the leg in an extension during this exercise."

14. Backfalls

"These falls must never be done unless you are prepared for them and have done them a great, great many times."

    a.   Preparation: two feet on the floor, sitting, deep contraction and release

    b.   Fall to the floor

"All falls are into the body—into yourself. The force of the movement returns the body to its original position from the fall."

    c.   With half turn on contraction

15. Sitting square front, heels off the floor
    a.   Contraction to back on hip, release to front
    b.   With raised arms
    c.   With spiral
    d.   With extension of the back leg on the rise
    e.   With strike (*battement*) of the leg to wide Second Position
    f.   Adding quarter and half turns

16. Sitting Fourth Position and rising to front
    a.   On four counts
    b.   On three counts
    c.   On two counts, lifting head
    d.   Into a spiral turn

Variation: with leg extension on contraction and release placing leg on floor.

"All of these falls (exercises 14–16) are performed with the pelvis up and under. The movement starts in the pelvis in the fall and in the return. The speed with which the falls are performed depends upon how early and carefully you were prepared for them."

17. Back contraction with crossed ankles (spine to the floor up to the shoulders)

"In dance, each time, it may be a mystical or religious con-
notation that you feel, but principally it is the body exalting in
its strength and its own power."

    a.   With elbows pressed together, hands toward the ceiling
    b.   With both legs extended front on the rise
    c.   With arms wrapped around the back of the waist
    d.   With arms opening to Second Position
    e.   Rising onto both knees at the end

18. Variation with one foot across the knee, on the floor, over
    the leg in front in Fourth Position
    a.   With arms extended
    b.   With the front foot extended
    c.   With a quarter turn onto the hip lying on the floor
    d.   Contraction over to elbows
    e.   Into Fourth Position
    f.   With turn on knees to sitting position

19. Sitting in Fourth Position
    a.   Contract and release with feet off the floor
    b.   With a quarter turn
    c.   With a leg extension front, then back

20. Leg extensions to the side (from backfalls as in the preced-
    ing exercises)
    a.   Leg extension to the back
    "There is no substitute for muscular strength in the body."
    b.   With a rise onto one knee and a turn as the leg extends
        to the side
    c.   With a complete backfall and rise onto one knee as the
        leg extends to the side

21. Rise onto one hand in contraction
    a.   Release to sit on hip
    b.   End in leg extension side

"No matter what the desire, there is nothing but training
that will accomplish these movements. The safety in doing these
exercises is within the movement itself."

22. Sitting in Second Position
    a. Release to lifted knees, heels on the floor
    "The waist stays still."
    b. Release with extension of the feet, back in spiral
23. High contraction to front and side
    a. With leg extension side
    b. With release to backbend
    c. With pitch to floor
    Variation: with rise to knees, contraction, and rise to knees
    in backbend.
24. Knee across front
    a. Backfall
    b. With rise to standing position, contraction to floor
    "Always return to center. So be it."

KNEES

Graham had a great deal to say about work on the knees. She
constantly emphasized that the leg muscles surrounding the knee
must be strong enough to take the weight off the bones of the
knee: "The muscles of the legs must be strong, and these exercises have nothing to do with the knees themselves."

Involved in the safety of performing exercises on the knees
is the manner in which attention is paid to their execution: "In
all exercises on the knees, whether a dancer does just one or
150, the execution must be exactly the same each time."

"The body has a lovely animal logic. It is the duty, the joy,
and the desire of each generation of dancers to discover more
deeply all of its meanings."

1. On one knee in Fourth Position (kneeling on one knee)

"All these exercises must be done slowly and with great concentration. The weight is held in the center of the body during
all of these movements," or returned to the center after a lunge,
tilt, or pitch.
    a. Quarter turn to back extension
    b. *Plié* to Second (leg opposite kneeling side is placed in
        Second Position, foot on the floor, then the *plié* is
        executed)

c. Change to other side (two knees together, then change)
d. To Second Position with body tilt (as in 1b., with tilt)
e. Change (two knees together to change sides)
f. With body tilt
g. Change with tilt of the body
h. With turn into contraction, sit
i. With lunge out
j. Change on knees
k. With lunge onto front leg
l. With pitch fall to elbows
m. With contraction, release on lunge
n. Pitch to elbows, Fourth Position turn
o. Contraction to sit

2. On one knee
   a. Contract to backfall, release to front and up to one knee
   b. Same, changing knees on release
   c. Travel back on the fall

3. On two knees
   a. Spiral contraction into sit, spiral release to rise

"Everything grows on a spiral." Meaning that there is a lift in the twist of the body as if to lift the body as it turns, not separately—lift then twist.

Variation: into back, "hips remain firm."

4. Strikes (*battements*) to the side in contraction
   a. Foot is placed on the floor to the side on the heel
   b. With spiral contraction and release into roll on the back, into strikes
   c. Ending with a sit on the hip, both legs extended to the side

5. Traveling crawls on the knee in contraction
   a. With deep sit, roll onto the knee as the other foot is placed on the floor to support the weight; then roll is repeated onto second knee as first leg supports the weight. The crawl is always supported by one foot on the floor
   b. Change on knees, using the same knee, crawling on one side

    c.   Crawls in a circle, one foot crossing over the knee
6. On one knee
    a.   Rise up from one knee onto the front foot in a tilt
    b.   Rise up onto one foot from one-knee position with a spiral in the body on the rise
    c.   Rise up with the back leg off of the floor in *attitude*
7. Exercise on six counts (begin kneeling on two knees); sometimes called a "hinge" as the body swings back and forth on the knees, torso straight
    a.   On six (body arches back as hands are placed on ankles)
    b.   With roll, straight back falling side, on back and up the other side
    c.   With backfall, falling straight back
Variation: with backfall and roll, falling backwards rolling on side to original "hinge" position*.

STANDING CENTER WORK

1. Standing with heels together, slightly turned-out feet
    a.   Two *demi-pliés*
    b.   With contraction "breathing throughout"
2. *Demi-pliés* in First, Second, Fourth, and Fifth Positions (arms slightly away from the body; head turned to the side of the front foot in Fourth Position; body has a slight twist)

    The exercise sometimes includes a rise to *demi-pointe* as the knees straighten; or the *demi-plié* may be executed on *demi-pointe* from the start. As in all exercises, the teacher decides upon the needs of the class. In *demi-pointe*, Graham says "it is a position of waiting to move."

3. Brushes (*battements*, on the floor, to 45 degrees; to 90 degrees)

---

* It will be noted by students of the Pilates Method—a series of rehabilitating and strengthening exercises created by Joe Pilates in the early 1920s—that some of Graham's exercises on the floor and knees are similar to Pilates'.
    Graham, like many dancers, became a life-long devotee of the Pilates Method and continued to perform Pilates-like exercises under the direction of her personal therapist, Robert Fitzgerald, intermittently throughout her life.
    Although no imitation of the Pilates exercises was intended by Graham, they appear in a transformed manner incorporated into the syllabus for their lengthening and strengthening value.

These *battement* exercises (3–10) are given at the discretion of the teacher as to sequence. "The dancer's time is spent not only in training the body, but in getting to know what it is capable of doing. The laws of the use of the body are as strict as the laws of architecture."

    a.   From First Position, one in four counts; two in two counts; eight ending in *demi-plié*; repeat to the other side; to the side

"The torso is held and the hips do not move; point from the sole of the foot."

    b.   In a faster tempo, sixteen ending in *demi-plié*; repeat to the other side

4. Parallel brushes, four on each leg to 45 degrees; four to 90 degrees

5. Contraction preparation and shift to brush side at 90 degrees, alternating

6. In parallel position, brush front and side, to 45 degrees and 90 degrees with contraction, two times each direction and height, ending with *demi-plié* between changes to other side

7. Quick brushes front, side, back, side on the floor, and then off the floor ending in *demi-plié* in four counts; other side

8. Brushes to side using given arm positions (front or back)
    a.   Ending in *demi-plié* and executed in *demi-plié*
    b.   With tilt of body toward leg, then away from leg
    c.   Repeat both sides in contraction

9. Brushes with turns (on the floor, rotating on the side of the supporting leg)

"The inner thigh muscles work to make this movement smooth."

10. Brushes with arms (First to Second) with a spiral toward the working leg; then away from the working leg; in eight counts, then four times in two counts

11. Turns with the working foot in *coupé* position (on the ankle) closing in Fifth Position front, then closing in Fifth Position back. To complete one turn, the first *coupé* closes front without a turn; then a quarter turn is executed with the next *coupé* closing back. (The turn is performed on the foot's sole of the supporting leg when the other foot is in *coupé* position).

By alternating closing front and back, the turn is completed
in five *coupés*

   a.   Turns with the working leg in *passé* (at the front of the
knee of the supporting leg) five times closing front and
back as in the preceding exercise

   b.   With a *plié* at the end of each quarter turn

12. High contraction in *grand plié* ending in *élevé* to *demi-pointe*

   a.   In First Position; in Second Position; in Fourth Position;
in Fifth Position

Variation: with spiral and full circle of arms, ending in *relevé*
(half-pointe). "This variation should never be taught unless
the classic version has been mastered."

BARRE WORK

Barre work contains extensive stretching ending in *élevés*—a rise
to the *demi-pointe*. Although the syllabus refers to a *relevé*—a
spring to the *demi-pointe*—the movement, as it is executed in a
controlled and smooth tempo, is closer to an *élevé* than a spring,
or *relevé*. The tempo throughout is a slow 4/4.

  1. *Demi-plié* facing the barre in First Position (approximate) with
a spiral (lean) directly side, opposite arm up; end in *élevé*
with two arms up; reverse spiral on next *demi-plié*. Then execute the same exercise with *grande pliés* in eight counts

"The spiral is performed without changing the placement
of the hips; the knees are free. The exercise is primarily for the
inside muscles of the legs, not only for the outside muscles."

  2. a.   Extension to the barre: The working leg performs a
développé from a *passé* position and opens above the barre
and is lowered gently onto the barre; then lifted off the
barre in sixteen counts

     b.   Variation (with *plié*): perform the same exercise with a
plié as the leg remains on the barre; opposite arm up

     c.   Variation: with a slide towards the same side as the leg
on the barre; ending in *demi-plié* then *élevé* upon return
to the right-angle position

"This all must be done gradually."

3. Variation with knee vibration (turned in, then out): The working leg performs a *développé* to the side from *passé* position turned in; then is turned out and extended to the side (knee vibration); then the supporting leg rises to *demi-pointe* and the body turns (in *fouetté*) away from the raised leg thus becoming an *arabesque*

4. As in exercise 3, with balances in the side extension and *arabesque*
   a. As in exercise 3, with contraction on knee vibration, release on turning out

Exercise 4 is given at the discretion of the teacher, taking into account the physical limitations of the students.

5. Brushes (*grand battements*) in a series to the side
   "The leg must be held for one second at the highest point."
   a. On the floor; to 45 degrees; to 90 degrees; as high as possible; two each in sixteen counts

6. Brushes with one hand on the barre, from First Position
   a. Three *grand battements* (brushes) front; *passé* to extension front in *plié*; *passé* to *tendu* on the floor and *battement* from *tendu* (toe is on the floor in *tendu*)
   c. Same exercise to the side extension
   d. Same to the back
   e. Reverse series beginning brushes back

7. Extensions (*grand battements*) to percussive music, with the accent at the height of the position
   "Extensions are an endless part of the dancer's vocabulary." This series of exercises is similar to a *grand adagio* at the barre and as given by the teacher may include *attitude* positions and turning toward and away from the barre in the big poses—*attitude* or *arabesque*.
   a. Facing the barre, extend to the side on *demi-pointe*
   b. With same-side arm raised
   c. With opposite arm raised

8. With one hand on the barre and turning quickly toward the barre to execute the exercise on the other side
   a. With *grand rond de jambe* (half circle of the leg at waist level) from 90 degrees front to *arabesque*; in reverse; and

en cloche—with a bell-like swing from high front to high back

9. Off-center *battements* with prances: tilts opposite the raised leg; some from *développé*—as given—and in *relevé*

10. Knee vibrations as *grand rond de jambe*
   a.   Waist-high extensions front to side; side to *arabesque*; full half-circle; with *relevés* as given

11. Preparation for hinges (slightly bent knees with the body on a straight line from knees to head)
   a.   In parallel position, *demi-plié*, lean backwards while holding onto the barre; push through the body to the upright position. This exercise sometimes ends with bounces

"Push through the body, but never through the knees."

12. Hinge to the ground with one hand on the barre pushing up through the body, "never through the knees"
   a.   With a quick drop (heels are off the floor in all hinges)

13. Full fall to floor using one hand on the barre as preparation for falls in the center. Fall is through the contraction preceding the fall; bounce is incorporated into the rise

14. "Bird" *pliés*

"The weight is carried high in the body." Arms are to the side like a bird's wings.
   a.   With the feet parallel, a deep *plié* is performed, then a swivel is executed after a contraction and the rise is to *demi-pointe* as the body completes a half turn
   b.   The same exercise in Fourth Position (similar to *temps lié*, but with a deep *plié*)
   c.   Variation: a rise with a straight back leg. In Fourth Position, with the body parallel to the floor

15. Variations on the positions of the rise
   a.   In Fourth Position as in exercise 14, ending with a lift of the back leg, body parallel to the floor
   b.   Lifting the leg and adding a *rond de jambe* as the supporting leg does a *demi-plié* (heel down); extension ends side
   c.   As in 15b., with a tilt opposite the raised leg

d. As in 15b., with no tilt and *rond de jambe* ending front in *plié*, close Fifth Position, turn, and execute on the opposite side

16. Preparation for turns (turns are in *passé* with the supporting foot slightly off the floor but not in *demi-pointe*)

a. Turn (pivot) from Second Position *plié* to right or left leg in *passé*

b. Same in Fourth Position

c. Combination: two preparations (no turn); two with a quarter turn; one in half turn; two in a full turn; change sides

17. Preparation for turns from Second to Fourth Position in a lunge

a. *Plié* in Second with *passé* preparation, no turn

b. Same with quarter turn (supporting foot does not rise to *demi-pointe*)

c. Turn half circle

d. Full turn (*passé* and quarter turn, heel on floor as in 17b., above)

CENTER

This series may be done as two preparations; two quarter turns; one half turn; two full turns. Change to other side.

1. Circular walk with spiral turns (walking on a diagonal, upstage left to downstage right)

a. As a preparation using *temps lié* (shifting from one position to another in Second or Fourth through *plié*). In a series: two preparations for a turn in low *arabesque*; two in quarter turn; one in half turn; two in full turns ending in a held balance

"The turn is done in a spiral" (a slight lean toward the direction of the turn).

b. Variation: with a pitch into *attitude*—two in preparation; two with full turns, hold ending in balance (a pitch finds the body parallel to the ground)

    c.   Variation: with a pitch into *arabesque* ending in *penchée* (full lowering of the body—nose to knee) on a straight supporting leg

    d.   With a step onto *demi-pointe* in *attitude* and pitch; two steps back and repeat to the other side (no turn)

    e.   Same as 1d., with two half turns

    f.   Same as 1d., with two full turns

    g.   Same as 1d., in a triplet walk (six counts) with a turn

    h.   Same as 1d., in four-count walk, turning in three counts

2. This section may be likened to *adagio* combinations, because of the control required in the transfer of weight

    a.   Preparations: *demi-plié* "pull" (tilt slightly) to side in First Position; lunge to Fourth Position and transfer leg in *tendu* to Second Position and balance with leg at 90 degrees in Second Position. No arms are used in this preparation

    b.   *Plié* in Second Position; raise leg to 90 degrees; return to First Position (Do twice, then change sides)

    c.   Repeat arms side, from Fourth Position front and back

"The shifting of the weight forces the body to take the relative position."

    d.   *Plié* in Second; shift weight to one side with foot in *passé* position (toes to knee of supporting leg); change sides, completing this series twice on each side

    e.   Same as in 2d., in *passé* from Fourth Position back; twice, change sides

    f.   *Plié* in Second Position, *passé*, *plié* in Fourth Position back, full turn with foot in *passé* (supporting leg is on quarter-*pointe* during the turn); once each side

"The weight of the body is exactly over the big ankle bone when the foot is in *passé*." Hip on supported side is directly over the ankle.

    g.   *Plié* in Second Position, shift weight to 90 degrees in *arabesque*, *rond de jambe* to Second Position, *rond de jambe* again to *arabesque* (*rond de jambe* on straight supporting leg); change on sixth count

Variation: exercise may be done as *grand battement* to Second and into *arabesque* beginning in Second Position *plié*

h.   Turn with feet in First Position, no arms; complete twice on each side (*demi-plié* in First Position gives force for the turn)

i.   Same turn in First Position as in 2h., but performed in Second Position *plié* with arms at right angles (elbows toward the ceiling); perform twice

j.   Same turn as 2h., with arms held slightly to the side from Fourth Position back; complete twice

k.   From Second Position preparation into First Position with *chassé* (triplet) to Fourth back; perform twice; change

l.   Add turn to First Position; perform twice; change

m.   Add turn from Fourth Position; perform twice; change

n.   A combination of 2k.–m.; complete twice to each side

A general word must be said here in order to understand the direction of the turns. When the right foot is in *passé* and the turn is to the right, the turn is *en dehors*—away from the body. When the same position is assumed, but the turn is to the left, the turn is *en dedans*—toward the body. The position of the foot does not determine the direction of the turn. "Away from" or "toward" the body are the directions for the turn.

3.   From Second Position *plié*, the leg lifts to Second Position at 90 degrees with the arms in "declaration" or open slightly to the front. (Called "presenting the movement" in ballet terminology)

a.   Add a contraction in the Second Position at 90 degrees

b.   Add a slow turn (*promenade*) in Second Position at 90 degrees; once each side, finish in *relevé*

4.   Contraction in First Position opening to Second at 90 degrees

a.   With a quarter turn in First opening to Second; twice in quarter turn; once in half turn; twice in full turns with feet parallel, heel of the turning foot slightly raised

"You don't copy these movements, you feel them."

5.   Contraction in Second *plié*; release into turn in Second Position, quarter turn twice; then half turn once; one full turn twice

6. With brushes (small *battements* on the floor) twice in Second Position, change to Fourth Position back and turn in First toward the body (*en dedans*); use the contraction on the turn

   a.   Add a release and tilt in the body

7. Same as exercise 6, with foot in *passé* with contraction from Second and Fourth Positions

"The Fourth Position is a classic position in Asia as well as in the West."

   a.   Add a tilt of the body

8. With preparation on Second in *plié*, shift to a side tilt and turn in Second Position in *relevé*; do the same from Fourth Position holding a balance at the end of each turn

   a.   With contraction on turn

   b.   End in a fall to the floor, instead of a balance

9. Split falls

   a.   *Tendu* side, split to the floor, body leans to the floor, leg comes around to Fourth Position front, rise, *temps lié* (transfer weight) to become Fourth Position, half turn

   b.   "Stagger" (Fourth Position to Second Position as if staggering), *tendu* to split side; same recovery as in 9a.

   c.   With *développé* to the side and a sit to the floor, contraction as feet come together in parallel position and the body does a rise

10. Knee vibrations

"These are called knee vibrations. In reality, they are like *rond de jambe*." Various arm patterns may be given for these movements and the contraction-release principle is also added.

   a.   From *passé*, turn the knee in (across the supporting leg), out, into *développé* side, and *rond de jambe* to *attitude*

Variation: turn the knee in, out, to *attitude*.

"This movement represents joy or anger, frustration: 'Shall I walk, or shall I not walk?' "

   b.   Starting low to the floor with the foot of the working leg no longer on the knee of the supporting leg, but separated by several inches; turn in and out with the supporting leg in *plié* several times as the body rises; the working leg ends in *attitude*; twelve counts

    c.   Knee in quasi-*passé* to the side as in 10a., remains in this position as the foot is thrown front-side-back; the movement ends in Second Position at 90 degrees; twelve counts

    d.   Combination of movements as in 10a.–c., with back movement ending on the outer thigh on floor, followed by a roll on the back and rising on one leg in *attitude*

    e.   Same as 10d., rising in Second Position to the side

11. From a parallel position, *grand battement* with a flexed foot front, four times, increasing in height; opposite arm pushes forward, ends on shoulder; finish with a half turn

    a.   With *battements* front and Second; four times reaching Second on the count of three (3/4 tempo)

    b.   In a handstand, beat and recover to upright position once forward, once side, eight times on three as in 3/4 tempo

The handstand is supported on one hand, elbow straight; the body is straight with legs overhead in parallel position. One leg beats or bounces off the other. The recovery is accomplished by placing one leg in Fourth Position front with bent knee onto floor and returning to an upright position. This movement is not a "walkover."

    c.   The handstand movement may be given in combinations to the front or to the side

12. *Rond de jambe* front to back while bending the supporting leg until the movement is on the floor, eight times on the "and-one" count. (Similar to movement in *Night Journey*)

Combinations from Graham dances are sometimes given in the class, such as: *American Document* step: *glissades* and small *emboîtés* (*coupé* away from the ankle), all to the front. The counts are: six, seven, six, seven, two for the combination.

13. Preparation for sitting from various positions

"The weight in all sits to the floor moves down through the center of the body."

    a.   From Fourth Position, a *grand plié* is executed to a sit on the floor as the back foot rotates so that the weight is on the outer thigh; rise on the supporting leg—front foot

b.   Same as 13a., with a contraction on the sit

14. In wide Second Position and straight legs, fall to the front using the hands for support; the body is rotated (right or left) to permit a roll on the back; rise on either foot

15. Beginning with two *grand battements* front and a *rond de jambe* to Second, the body lunges toward the leg in Second; as the other leg is thrown back the body rotates on the back leg; rise

   a.   Same as 15, with a *rond de jambe* going directly to Fourth Position back and a rise ending in a side extension
   b.   Add a contraction to 15
   c.   Add a contraction to 13a.
   d.   Add a contraction to the sit and rise in a side extension (15a.)

16. *Grands battements* to the side; *rond de jambe* front to *attitude* position; sit; rise in the same *attitude* position

17. Pitch turns (*penchée* positions in *attitude* or *arabesque*)

   ". . . with a deep contraction as preparation and a high release on the rise."

   a.   Preparation with two steps and *arabesque*, pitch, no turn
   b.   Preparation and full turn in eight counts on a straight leg
   c.   Full turn on four counts; two full turns in three counts (The sole of the foot remains on the floor as it pivots, the heel raises slightly to accommodate the turn)

18. Pitch turns on one knee. Walk into contraction in Fourth Position (or Second); raise a leg into a small *attitude* or *arabesque* position and turn on the front knee (it is placed gently on the floor); recover by swinging the back raised leg front to Fourth Position and rise

   "The knees are not in danger because of the preparation in the earlier exercises. The weight is up into the body itself, never down into the knees."

   a.   Add a side extension
   b.   Standing in side extension, pitch turn with the head almost touching the knee of the supporting leg

19. Prances (march-like steps with knees lifted high or low as given) through a roll from flat to *demi-pointe* and a small push off the floor—cat-like

"These prances and turns are done on both sides," and are usually performed on the diagonal.

a. Preparation: hold each prance for four counts, four times; two counts, four times; and alternating feet for sixteen counts

b. Two prances with sharp *passé* and a tilt toward the lifted foot

c. Two prances with a half turn in *passé*

d. Two prances with full turns

e. Two prances with a side extension on *demi-pointe* into a full turn

20. Jumps from two feet to two feet, and to one foot (*sissonnes*)

a. Big jump from parallel position to Second, ending with one leg in Second Position; close to parallel; jump in First

b. Big jumps in First with bent knees, soles touching

c. Continuous big jumps in Second Position

d. Jumps with parallel feet

e. Two jumps to the side, ending on two feet (*sissonne fermé*)

f. Two jumps with movement backwards, and with forward movement

21. Jumps from parallel First Position to a turned-out position in the air, knees side, soles together at the crest of the jump and landing in First Position

a. From parallel First Position, jump with one foot in *passé* position, the other straight out in a lowered Second Position; repeat to the other side. Jump continuously

22. *Aegisthus* jump: from parallel position, jump continuously with both legs in *attitude derrière* (backwards)

TRAVELING ACROSS THE FLOOR

1. Walks

a. Simple walk across the floor on diagonal: "These are brushes." The foot passes along a straight line, the body and head turn slightly

b. The arms swing on the fourth count

c.   Variation: walk with knee bent, foot raised in back

d.   Walk two steps and step on heel into a low *arabesque;* roll down to the flat foot

e.   Step on each count in *arabesque*

f.   Two *arabesque* steps, changing direction with a half turn on the second *arabesque;* do two in the opposite direction from the first two steps in the same pattern

g.   Two *arabesque* steps with contraction to floor, head back

"You are held by the upper back and the thighs."

h.   Four walks and hold balance, bent knee, working foot in *passé* position

i.   Four walks and quick *développé* side

Variation: *grand battement* front and swing through First Position as the body does a half turn (*fouetté*); and the same leg does a *grand battement* to the front. (The movement is bell-like in the legs)

Variation: same exercise as in 1i., with *grands battements* back

2. Low walks with back leg dragging, knees slightly bent, arms swinging and with increasing speed. At full speed, this movement is known as the *Diversion of Angels* run

3. Triplets

"The weight is held as in flight."

a.   Three steps: first count, step in *demi-plié;* second step is higher; third, same as second step. (The *plié* and rise are slight, giving the impression of a slight accent on the one count as in a waltz)

b.   A turn on every second step (without, then with arms). The working leg is 45 degrees in front

c.   A turn on each step (without, then with arms)

d.   Turn as in 3c., and hold on fourth count

e.   Same as in 3c., holding a balance (rise to *demi-pointe* on fourth count)

f.   Two walks and an *arabesque* on the heel on the third count

4. Diagonal walks

a.   Walks in Second Position to Fourth—step right in Second, step left in Fourth (right foot held at the ankle in back)

    b.   Same as in 4a., with foot held in *passé* back

    c.   Same as in 4a., with arm swing opposite raised foot

    d.   Same as in 4a., with a slight jump, without arm

    e.   Same as in 4a., with slight jump adding opposite-arm movement

5. Skips

    a.   Alternating legs

    b.   Skip on same leg, with step on opposite leg between skips

6. Skips in large poses

    a.   Step, step, *sauté* in *attitude* front, then in *attitude* back

    b.   Same as in 6a., with *grand jeté* on third count

    c.   Same as in 6a., with *grand jeté* on the same leg on second count

7. Hops while executing a low *rond de jambe*, back to front

    a.   While turning

8. Step-draws (*glissade*-like steps)

    a.   Slow *glissade* right and left ending in a *coupé* (foot at the ankle back or front)

    b.   With small 45-degree *battement* followed by a *glissade* or "draw"

    c.   Same as in 8a., with *relevé* on supporting leg, *passé* on working leg, ending in *glissade*

    d.   *Arabesque*, swing front, *fouetté* (in *fouetté*, the leg remains placed and the body turns—in *rond de jambe*, the body remains placed and the leg executes the movement); and draw or *glissade* (same leg movement)

9. *Seraphic Dialogue* strikes

    a.   *Battement* to Second, "draw" working leg to *passé* and turn, movement alternates

    b.   *Battement* side with half turn each step

10. Pitch (*penchée*) *attitude* on right, half turn, step on left with right in Second Position completing second half of turn

11. Contraction and release turns in Second with pitch

    "It's something you learn and something you develop."

    a.   In Second Position, contract and release facing diagonal corner and traveling

b.   With a turn in Second facing upstage, changing sides to Second Position facing downstage

c.   Contraction on half turn; release on next half turn

d.   Same as 11c., ending in Fourth Position lunge

e.   Same as 11c., with slight pitch forward in Fourth

12. Contraction drops performed traveling in the diagonal

a.   Turns in *attitude* in contraction

b.   Same as 12a., ending in sit to floor

c.   Same as 12a., ending in sit and turn on floor

13. Turns with hips parallel in *attitude*

14. *Arabesque* turns contracting into *attitude*, without, then with, a turn

15. Walking backwards in contraction-release "profile"

16. Traveling in diagonal with *grand battement* front in contraction

a.   *Gospel of Eve* contraction: *grand battement* front, jump into *attitude* turn (pitch)

17. *Cave of the Heart* turn: in *arabesque*, pitched, with variation opening to Second. Turn on the one count, step, step

"This turn can be done in a joyous manner or may indicate jealousy or anger."

18. *Electra* turns: a series of *arabesque* turns ending in Second, left leg bent when turn is on right side

19. *Diversion of Angels* turn: Traveling *attitude* turn with strike into *attitude*

20. *Clytemnestra* turn: *Arabesque* turn on heel finishing with forward contraction; palm of hand on forehead of supporting side in "anguish"

21. Circular walks

a.   Back leg lifts to Second Position, falls front, repeat other side

b.   Same as 21a., with *relevé* in Second Position and pitch *attitude* in *tombée* front

d.   Same as 21a., with two steps between

22. *Développés* in Second Position, *arabesque*, and front *tombée, plié*

ACROSS THE FLOOR IN DIAGONAL

1. Traveling prances (march in parallel position using the knee to raise each foot off the floor in the image of a prancing horse)
   a. Prancing across the floor in a diagonal
   b. With a strike (*battement*) to the floor on the eighth count
   c. With a small jump on the eighth count
   d. With changes of direction and a turn on the eighth count toward various directions: half, quarter, and full turns
   e. With a bend to the side on the seventh count in *passé*, to *attitude* back on the eighth count
   f. Prances to Fourth Position—jump on the tenth count
2. Jumps in Second Position with a tilt to the side on a given count
   a. Jumps with a tilt side, straight, other side
   b. Jumps in Second Position with a contraction to make the torso almost parallel with the floor
3. Bell jumps (*grand jeté*)
   a. Straight forward on the same leg
   b. With two steps between and alternating sides for jump
4. Jumps with an *arabesque* at a given count from prances
   a. Jumps into Second Position in contraction with hands touching feet (Cossack jump)
5. *Seraphic Dialogue* jump: jump with one leg in Second Position at 90 degrees side; step on raised leg; repeat in side pattern; arms between legs in jump, hands clasped
6. "Sparkle" jumps: *Arabesque sauté* jumps with two steps between—*arabesque* alternates, repeats in a series with arms shooting up on the *arabesque*
   a. Continuous *arabesque sautés* alternating sides, arms up on each *sauté*—jump
7. Traveling sits: step, step, sit (a crouch, both knees bent, buttocks not on the floor)
   a. With a small jump before the sit, rise with leg side, body in contraction

8. Traveling split/fall: 90-degree side jump with fall straight forward, hands breaking the fall
   a.   Big jump ending in a sit (crouch) instead of a fall forward
9. Split to side, fall forward, roll on side to back, and come up in Fourth Position; may be repeated as a traveling step

   Variations: front split, one leg bent, rise in *plié*, other leg in Second Position; same but rising in *arabesque*
10. *Diversion of Angels* jumps: prance-like *emboîtés* with leg raised higher in front—a series of small jumps alternating feet, body in contraction forward, arms to the side

    Variation: with feet raised in *emboîtés* back, body pitched forward or legs in *arabesque* jumps.
11. "Butterflies" are *emboîtés* back with step, step between. They may be imaged as *temps de flèche derrière* with two steps between
12. March jumps: continuous jumps into *attitude* back—or may be imaged as continuous *temps de flèche* on each leg—or as jumps into *attitude* back alternating legs and in contraction (from a parallel position)
13. *Diversion of Angels* step: jump in Second Position at 90 degrees with a tilt to the side, step, step. (All traveling steps may be executed separately, or continuously without two steps between)
14. Straight leg jumps: *grand battement* front with a jump, step, step
    a.   With a contraction and tilt forward to parallel-to-floor position
15. "Stranger" jump: a crouch with two knees up to the chest, body in contraction
16. "Stranger" with chasing run; traveling *Stranger* jump from parallel position
17. *Cortège of Eagles* jump: *sauté* in Second Position, land in *attitude* back
18. "Barrel" jumps: two knees up, arms back, "like jumping over something"
19. *Assemblé* front with parallel feet; land in *attitude* side—knee bent and parallel to hip
    a.   With contraction on the landing in *attitude*

    b.   "Bison" jump: front and back legs in *attitude* in the air—approached from a run, or step, step; land in *attitude* back

20. *Pas de chat* (without turning out) from four *emboîtés, pas de chat* on the five count

    a.   *Jeté* (brush side, land in modified *coupé*) four times, then *pas de chat*

    b.   *Pas de chats* with *jeté*, jumping onto front foot in combinations

    c.   "Stag" leap: big jump with front leg in *passé*, knee forward, back leg in *arabesque*: step, jump; step, jump. Exit step: two arms up or in Fourth Position

    Variation: a series of *emboîtés* and *pas de chats* with a turn.

21. *Primitive Mysteries* jumps: arms behind, body in crouch, series of *jeté* jumps front, leg in *attitude* back in landing

22. *Furies* jump: series of *grand jetés* across the floor with the left arm thrust forward; jump is on the same leg—fast exit

23. *Diversion of Angels* jump: from-the-floor jump in Second Position, fall to floor and hop into *attitude* from floor (with or without a turn)

24. Triplet combination: step, step, turn *à la seconde, sauté* on three—a traveling step

25. "Lake Placid" combination: a series of *jetés* (three), with a fall front on the chest, a rise *à la seconde*

26. Combination: contraction with leg *à la seconde*, swing raised leg behind supporting leg now in *plié*, roll on back, rise on same supporting leg in Second Position at 90 degrees, with or without *plié*. During roll on back, legs may be straight or bent, knees to the chest

27. Knee walks ("keep the upper body held high"): step, step, kneel on back leg, rise on next step; alternates in a traveling series

    a.   Continuously step, kneel

28. Knee *bourées: bourée* on knees sideways

    a.   *Bourée* front

29. Free series of falls: *passé* in contraction, *développé* side, *rond de jambe* to *attitude* back, fall on thigh of *attitude* leg, rise in given position

  a.   From kneeling position, body falls backward, roll on side. Knees come up to chest during roll on back, come up in given position

  b.   From *relevé* on supporting leg, other leg in *à la seconde*, fall and roll on back with rise in side *attitude*, hand on ankle

  c.   ''The simplest fall'': from parallel position, bend knees and contract forward, roll onto shoulders and come up on knees. During roll on back, legs may be straight or bent close to the chest

Appendix

MARTHA GRAHAM DANCE COMPANY, THE DANCERS, 1926–1990

Based and enlarged upon a list compiled by Louis Horst and Alice Helpern; omissions are an oversight.

1926–1929*

Thelma Biracree, 1926
Virginia Briton, 1929–1931
Hortense Bunsick, 1929–1931
Louise Creston, 1929–1934
Irene Emery, 1929–1930
Betty Macdonald, 1926–1930
Lillian Ray, 1929–1934
Kitty Reese, 1929–1930

Mary Rivoire, 1929–1933
Sylvia Rosenstein, 1929
Ethel Rudy, 1929–1934
Evelyn Sabin, 1926–1930
Rosina Savelli, 1926–1930
Lillian Shapero, 1929–1934
Sylvia Wasserstrom, 1929–1930
Ruth White, 1929–1932

* Thelma Biracree, Betty Macdonald, and Evelyn Sabin danced with Martha Graham in her first independent concert on April 18, 1926.

1930–1939*

Anita Alvarez, 1934–1939
Thelma Babitz, 1936–1939
Bonnie Bird, 1933–1937
Dorothy Bird, 1931–1937
Sydney Brenner, 1931–1933
Ethel Butler, 1933–1944
Grace Cornell, 1931
Merce Cunningham, 1939–1945
Jane Dudley, 1934–1946, 1953, 1970
Jean Erdman, 1938–1945, 1970, 1974–1976
Nelle Fisher, 1937–1941
Frieda Flier, 1936–1941
Nina Fonaroff, 1937–1946
Beatrice Gerson, 1931–1932
Ailes Gilmour, 1930–1933
Georgia Graham, 1931
Mattie Haim, 1931–1934
Elizabeth Halpern, 1938–1942
Natalie Harris, 1937–1939
Erick Hawkins, 1938–1950
Martha Hill, 1930–1931

Lil Liandre, 1934–1936
Marie Marchowsky, 1934–1940, 1944
Sophie Maslow, 1931–1944
Marjorie Mazia, 1936–1946
Lily Mehlman, 1931–1936
Freema Nadler, 1931–1932
Pauline Nelson, 1931–1933
May O'Donnell, 1932–1938, 1943–1953
Mary Raoin, 1932–1934
Florence Schneider, 1934–1936
Bessie Schönberg, 1930–1931
Catherine Selby, 1932
Elizabeth Sherbon, 1936–1940
Gertrude Shurr, 1930–1938
Kathleen Slanle, 1935–1938
Anna Sokolow, 1930–1938
Housely Stevens, Jr., 1938–1940
Martha Todd, 1931
Mildred Wile, 1934–1936
Joan Woodruff, 1930–1933

Workshop Group: Bennington College, 1935 **(Panorama)**
Miriam Blecher, Prudence Bredt, Nadia Chilkovsky, Evelyn Davis, Nancy Funston, Alice Gates, Mildred Glassberg, Mary Ann Goldwater, Marie Heghinian, Merle Hirsh, Gussie Kirshner, Edith Langbert, Naomi Lubell, Mary Moore, Helen Priest, Pearl Satlien, Muriel Stuart, Maxine Trevor, Theodora Weisner, Collin Wilsey, Marian Van Tuyl, Florence Verdon

Assistant Dance Group: 1938 **(American Document)**
Betty Bloomer, Jean Campbell, Charlotte Chandler, Betty Garrett, Miriam Korngold, Jane McLean, Kaya Rassell, Elizabeth Sherbon, Margaret Strater, Lillian Willis, Collin Wilsey, Mildred Wirt

1940–1949

Sara Aman, 1949–1950
Richard Aston, 1945
Barbara Bennion, 1949–1950
Dorothy Berea, 1948
Graham Black, 1946–1947

Barbara Bray, 1944
John Butler, 1943–1953
Nina Caiserman, 1944
David Campbell, 1940–1944
Robert Cohan, 1946–1969

---

* Ailes Gilmour is the sister of Isamu Noguchi; Georgia Graham, who died in 1989, was the sister of Martha Graham and was also a Denishawn dancer; Betty Bloomer is former First Lady Betty Ford

Nina Crown, 1942
Dorothea Douglas, 1946–1950
Eleanore Goff, 1949–1950
George Hall, 1940
Stuart Hodes, 1946–1958
Robert Horan, 1942–1944
Phyllis Kahan, 1944
Angela Kennedy, 1943–1948
Pearl Lang, 1941–1954, 1970–1978
Marie-Louise Louchheim,
    1949–1950
David Mann, 1945
Lili Mann, 1944

Helen McGehee, 1944–1972
Natanya Neumann, 1946–1953
Miriam Pander, 1944
Bertram Ross, 1949–1973
Mark Ryder, 1941–1949
Dale Sehnert, 1948
Joan Skinner, 1947–1949
William Swatzell, 1945
Douglas Watson, 1946
Ethel Winter, 1944–1968, 1973
Judith Yanus, 1949–1950
Yuriko, 1944–1967
David Zellmer, 1940–1946

1950–1959

Lillian Biersteker, 1954–1957
Patricia Birch, 1950–1970
Miriam Cole, 1952–1958
Donya Feuer, 1955
Paul Gannon, 1950
Ellen Graff, 1958–1962
Mary Hinkson, 1952–1973
Akiko Kanda, 1958–1962
Dorothy Krooks, 1952
Richard Kuch, 1958–1970
Christine Lawson, 1955
Linda Margolies (Hodes),
    1952–1969, 1975–1976
Camera McCosh, 1954
Gene McDonald, 1958–1968

Donald McKayle, 1955
Jack Moore, 1953
Carol Payne, 1958–1960
Luisa Pierce, 1954
Bette Shaler, 1958–1960
Lois Schlossberg, 1958–1960
Eileen Siegel, 1955–1958
Leslie Snow, 1953
Paul Taylor, 1955–1962
Glen Tetley, 1958
Matt Turney, 1952–1973
Ellen Van Der Hoeven, 1955
Dan Wagoner, 1958–1968
David Wood, 1953–1967

1960–1969

Hugh Appet, 1968–1970
Takako Asakawa, 1962–
Frank Ashley, 1969
Moss Cohen, 1965–1970
Robert Dodson, 1968–1969
Juliet Fisher, 1962–1967
Carol Fried, 1962–1967
Richard Gain, 1962–1970
James Gardner, 1960
Guillermo Gonzalez, 1968
Diane Gray, 1964–1979
Phyllis Gutelius, 1962–1977
Judith Hogan, 1967–1975
Yuriko Kimura, 1967–1985
Lynne Kothera, 1961–1962
Noemi Lapsezon, 1965–1969
Judith Leifer, 1967–1970

William Louther, 1964–1971
Jeanne Nuchtern, 1965
Ross Parkes, 1965–1975
Kenneth Pearl, 1967–1969
Robert Powell, 1960–1976
Peter Randazzo, 1962–1967
Lar Roberson, 1969–1973
Chase Robinson, 1968
Mable Robinson, 1962
Rachamin Ross, 1968
Gus Solomons, Jr., 1965
Nancy Stevens, 1960
Dawn Suzuki, 1968–1972
Marnie Thomas, 1960–1967
Olive Thompson, 1962–1969
Dudley Williams, 1960–1968

1970–1979

Thea Nerissa Barnes, 1979–
Mary Barnett, 1976
Fred Bratcher, 1976
Roger Briant, 1973
Charles Brown, 1978–1983
David Brown, 1978–1983
Jacqulyn Buglisi, 1977–
Terese Capucilli, 1979–
William Carter, 1973–1977
Holly Cavrell, 1973–1974
Jessica Chao, 1975–1976
David Chase, 1974–1977
Christine Dakin, 1976–
Ann DeGrange, 1972–1973
Mario Delamo, 1974–1978
Janet Eilber, 1972–1985
Ralph Farrington, 1975
Wesley Fata, 1976
Donlin Foreman, 1977–
Judith Garay, 1977–
Diana Hart, 1974–1977
Evind Harum, 1975
Linda Hayes, 1975–1976
Helen Jones, 1977–1988
Kevin Keenan, 1978–1983
Susan Kikuchi, 1978–1984
Sherry Linn, 1974

Peggy Lyman, 1973–
Daniel Maloney, 1973–1976
Susan McGuire, 1973–1976
Susan McLain, 1977–1983
Lucinda Mitchell, 1972–1978
Elisa Monte, 1974–1983
Traci Musgrove, 1972–1973
Ohad Naharin, 1975–1976
Eric Newton, 1973–1977
Bonnie Oda, 1974–1978, 1981
Olabayo, 1973
Carl Paris, 1973–1974
Jeanne Ruddy, 1977–1985
Philip Salvatori, 1978–1985
Barry Smith, 1975–1976
Peter Sparling, 1973–1987
Keiko Takeya, 1975–1976
Bert Terborgh, 1976–1983
Sharon Tyers, 1977–1980
Armgard von Dardeleben,
    1973–1976
Allen Von Hackendahl, 1978–1979
David Hatch Walker, 1970–1984
Shelley Washington, 1974–1976
Tim Wengerd, 1973–1985
George White, Jr., 1977–
Henry Yu, 1974–1977

Guest artists: *Margot Fonteyn, 1975–1977; Liza Minnelli, 1978–1980; Rudolf Nureyev, 1975–1984. Mary Collins, Sharon Filone, Salley Trammell, 1977, added for* Primitive Mysteries *performances.*

1980–1990

Tali Ben David, 1982
Mark Borneman, 1985–
Lyndon Branaugh, 1984–
Camile Brown, 1987–
Kathy Buccellato, 1986–
Mario Camacho, 1986–
Duane Cyrus, 1988–
Christopher Dolder, 1986–
Stephen Fant, 1980–
Floyd Flynn, 1986–
Sophie Giovanola, 1981–1986
Joyce Herring, 1982–
David Hochoy, 1982–1986

Laura Jimenez, 1988–
Debra Kanton, 1984–
Julian Littleford, 1984–
Peter London, 1988–
Teresa Maldonado, 1986–
Carol Mead, 1982–1985
Miguel Moore, 1984–1985
Jean-Louis Morin, 1980–1985
Anthony Morgan, 1982–1983
Miki Orihara, 1987–
Donald Prosch, 1980–1981
Pascal Rioult, 1986–
Steve Rooks, 1982–

Kenneth Scott, 1980
Maxine Sherman, 1983–
Andrea Smith, 1980–1983
Tom Smith, 1982–1984
Daniela Stasi, 1988–
Gregory Steward, 1984–1986
Kim Stroud, 1982–
Tancredo Tavares, 1988–
Kenneth Topping, 1985–

Helen Tran, 1984–
Denise Vale, 1984–
Larry White, 1980–1987
Kimberly Wisner, 1982–1984
Myra Woodruff, 1988–
Mina Yoo, 1980
Young-Ha Yoo, 1988–
Ed Zujkowski, 1982–1985

Guest Artists, *1987 gala: Rudolf Nureyev, Maya Plisetskaya, Mikhail Baryshnikov. 1988: Kathleen Turner* (American Document). *Lisa Barnett, Cheryl Crowley, Jean Ference, Lon Macdougal, Pamela Risenhoover, 1982, added for* Primitive Mysteries. *Emanuela Ciavarella, Vivien Eng, Katie Haltiwanger, Deborah Hanna, Lisa Ann Heath, Laura Jimenez, Naoko Katakami, Lone Kjaer Larsen, Daniela Stasi, Sheron Lynn Neverson, Noreen Pietri, Anne Westwick, Myra Woodruff, 1987, added for* Primitive Mysteries. *Silvana Eder, Vivien Eng, Adria Ferrali, Deborah Hanna, Laura Jimenez, Naoko Katakami, Lone Larsen, Sheron Neverson, Noreen Pietri, Alessandra Prosperi, Mira Rivera, Anne Westwick, 1988, added for* Celebration.

THE DANCES OF MARTHA GRAHAM

Martha Graham choreographed over 200 dances for the company she founded in 1926. In addition to this list of company dances, Graham choreographed an unknown number of dances when she was a member of the Denishawn Company in the 1920s, short dances for demonstrations at Bennington College in Vermont from 1934 to 1942 (she was artist-in-residence from 1942–1944), and dances for plays performed at the Neighborhood Playhouse in New York City in the 1930s and 1940s. This list is a revised and enlarged version of lists compiled by Louis Horst, Alice Helpern, and Don McDonagh.

1926, April 18, 48th Street Theatre, NYC

Chorale, César Franck, *Prelude, Chorale, Fugue*

Novelette, Robert Schumann, *Bunte Blätter*, Op. 99

Tänze, Franz Schubert

Intermezzo, Johannes Brahams, *Intermezzo, #18; Op. 119, #3*

Maid with the Flaxen Hair, Claude Debussy, *Preludes*, Book 1, #8

Arabesque #1, Claude Debussy

Clair de Lune, Claude Debussy, *Suite Bergamasque*

Danse Languide, Alexander Scriabin, Op. #5

Désir, Alexander Scriabin, Op. 57, #4

Deux Valses Sentimentales, Maurice Ravel, *Valses Nobles et Sentimentale, #2, #3*

Masques, Louis Horst, *Masques for Piano*

Trois Gnossiennes: Gnoissienne/Frieze/Tanagra, Erik Satie, *Trois Gnossiennes*

From a XII Century Tapestry, retitled a *Florentine Madonna*, Sergei Rachmaninoff

A Study in Lacquer, Marcel Bernheim

Danse Rococo, Maurice Ravel

The Three Gopi Maidens (excerpt from *The Flute of Krishna*), Cyril Scott

The Marionette Show, Eugene Goossens

Portrait—After Beltram Masses, retitled *Gypsy Portrait,* Manuel de Falla

1926, May 27, Kilbourne Hall, Rochester, NY

The Flute of Krishna, Cyril Scott

Suite from *Alceste,* Christopher Willibald von Gluck

Scène Javanaise, Louis Horst

Danza degli Angeli, Ermanno Wolf-Ferrari

Bas Relief, Cyril Scott

1926, August 20, Mariarden, Peterboro, NH

Ribands, Frédéric Chopin

1926, November 28, Klaw Theatre, NYC

Scherzo, Felix Mendelssohn, Op. 16, #2

Baal Shem, Ernest Bloch

La Soirée dans Grenade (retitled *The Moth*), Claude Debussy, from *Estampes*

Alt-Wien, Leopold Godowsky, arranged by Louis Horst

Three Poems of the East, Louis Horst

1926, Date and place of premiere unknown

Arabesque

Pictures in Melody

May Time in Kew (Valse)

Then and Now (Gavotte)

A Corner in Spain

A Dream in a Wax Museum (Dance of French Dolls)

A Forest Episode

1927, February 27, Guild Theatre, NYC

Peasant Sketches: Dance/Berceuse/In the Church, Vladimir Rebikov, Alexander Tansman, Peter Tchaikovsky
Tunisia: Sunlight in a Courtyard, Eduard Poldini
Lucrezia, Claude Debussy
La Canción Trágica, René Delfosse

1927, August 2, Anderson-Milton School, NYC

Arabesque #1 (revised), Claude Debussy
Valse Caprice, Cyril Scott, Op. 74, #7

1927, October 16, The Little Theatre, NYC

Spires, J. S. Bach, *Chorale: "Schwing dich auf zu deinem Gott"*
Adagio, retitled *Madonna,* George Frideric Handel, *Adagio* from *Second Suite*
Fragilité, Alexander Scriabin, Op. 51, #1
Lugubre, Alexander Scriabin, Op. 51, #2
Poème Ailé, Alexander Scriabin, Op. 51, #3
Tanzstück, Paul Hindemith, Op. 37
Danse, retitled *Revolt,* Arthur Honegger, from *Trois Pieces*
Esquisse Antique, Désiré Emile Inghelbrecht, from *Driades #2*
Ronde, Rhené-Baton, from *Au Pardon de Rumengol*

1927, December 10, Cornell University, Ithaca, NY

Scherza, Robert Schumann

1928, February 12, Civic Repertory Theatre, NYC

Chinese Poem, Louis Horst

1928, April 22, The Little Theatre, NYC

Trouvères (Return of Spring/Complaint/A Song, Frank and Gay), Charles Koechlin

Immigrant (Steerage Strike), Joseph Slavenski, from *Suite Aus dem Balkan*

Poems of 1917, Leo Ornstein

Fragments (Tragedy/Comedy), Louis Horst

Resonances (Matins/Gamelan/Tocsin), Gian Francesco Malipiero

Tanagra, Erik Satie

1929, January 20, Booth Theatre, NYC

Dance, Arthur Honegger

Three Florentine Vases, Domenico Zipoli

Four Insincerities (Petulance/Remorse/Politeness/Vivacity), Serge Prokofiev, *Visions fugitive*, Op. 22, #14, #12, #6, #11

Chants Magics (Farewell/Greetings), Federico Mompou

Two Variations (Country Lane/City Street), Alexander Gretchaninoff, *Sonatina*, Op. 110, #1

1929, January 24, Bennett School, Millbrook, NY

Figure of a Saint, George Frideric Handel

1929, March 3, Booth Theatre, NYC

Resurrection, Tibor Harsányi

Adolescence, Paul Hindemith, Op. 37

Danza, Darius Milhaud

1929, April 14, Booth Theatre, NYC

Visions of the Apocalypse (Theme and Variations), Herman Reutter

Moment Rustica, Francis Poulenc, *Sonata Rustique*

Sketches from the People, Julien Krein, *Preludes*, Op. 5, #4, #2, #7

Heretic, anonymous Breton folksongs

1929, Date and place of premiere unknown

Sarabande and Courante, J. S. Bach

Prelude in Black, Song in White, Paul Hindemith

1930, January 8, Maxine Elliott's Theatre, NYC

Prelude to a Dance, retitled *Salutation*, Arthur Honegger, *Counterpoint #1*

Two Chants (Futility, Ecstatic Song), Ernst Krenek, *Piano Sonata*, Op. 59, #2

Lamentation, Zoltan Kodály, Op. 3, #2

Project in Movement for a Divine Comedy, no music

Harlequinade, Ernst Toch, Op. 32

1931, February 2, Craig Theatre, NYC

Two Primitive Canticles, Heitor Villa-Lobos

Primitive Mysteries (Hymn to the Virgin/Crucifixus/Hosanna), Louis Horst

Rhapsodics (Song/Interlude/Dance), Béla Bartók

Bacchanale, Wallingford Riegger

Dolorosa, Heitor Villa-Lobos

1931, December 6, Martin Beck Theatre, NYC

Dithyrambic, Aaron Copland, *Piano Variations*

Serenade, Arnold Schoenberg

Incantation, Heitor Villa-Lobos

1932, February 28, Guild Theatre, NYC

Ceremonials, Lehman Engel

1932, June 2, Mendelssohn Theatre, Ann Arbor, MI

Offering, Heitor Villa-Lobos

Ecstatic Dance, Tibor Harsányi

Bacchanale #2, Wallingford Riegger

1932, November 20, Guild Theatre, NYC

Prelude, Carlos Chavez

Dance Songs (*Ceremonial/Morning Song/Satyric Festival Song, Song of Rapture*), Imre Weisshaus
Chorus of Youth—Companions, Louis Horst

1933, February 20, Fuld Hall, Newark, NJ

Tragic Patterns (*Chorus for Supplicants, Chorus for Maenads/Chorus for Furies*), Louis Horst

1933, May 4, Guild Theatre, NYC

Elegiac, Paul Hindemith, *Music for Unaccompanied Clarinet*
Ekstasis, Lehman Engel

1933, November 19, Guild Theatre, NYC

Dance Prelude, Nikolas Lopatnikoff
Frenetic Rhythms (*Three Dances of Possession*), Wallingford Riegger

1934, February 18, Guild Theatre, NYC

Transitions (*Prologue, Saraband/Pantomime/Epilogue*), Lehman Engel
Phantasy (*Prelude/Musette/Gavotte*), Arnold Schoenberg

1934, February 25, Guild Theatre, NYC

Celebration, Louis Horst
Four Casual Developments, Henry Cowell

1934, April 22, Alvin Theatre, NYC

Intégrales (*Shapes of Ancestral Wonder*), Edgard Varèse

1934, November 11, Guild Theatre, NYC

Dance In Four Parts (*Quest/Derision/Dream/Sportive Tragedy*), George Antheil
American Provincials (*Act of Piety/Act of Judgment*), Louis Horst

1935, February 10, Guild Theatre, NYC

Praeludium #1, Paul Nordoff
Course, George Antheil

1935, April 28, Guild Theatre, NYC

Perspectives (*Frontier, Marching Song*), Louis Horst, *Frontier;* Lehman Engel, *Marching Song*

1935, August 14, Vermont State Armory, Bennington, VT

Panorama (*Theme of Dedication/Imperial Theme/Popular Theme*), Norman Lloyd

1935, November 10, Guild Theatre, NYC

Formal Dance, retitled *Praeludium #2*, David Diamond

1935, April 7, Philharmonic Auditorium, Los Angeles, CA

Imperial Gesture, Lehman Engel
Panic (*Choral Movement*)

1936, February 23, Guild Theatre, NYC

Horizons, Louis Horst
Salutation, Lehman Engel

1936, December 20, Guild Theatre, NYC

Chronicle, Wallingford Riegger

1937, July 30, Vermont State Armory, Bennington, VT

Opening Dance, Norman Lloyd
Immediate Tragedy, Henry Cowell

1937, December 19, Guild Theatre, NYC

Deep Song, Henry Cowell

1937, December 26, Guild Theatre, NYC

American Lyric, Alex North

1938, August 6, Vermont State Armory, Bennington, VT

American Document, Ray Green

1939, December 27, St. James Theatre, NYC

Columbiad, Louis Horst
"Every Soul Is a Circus," Paul Nordoff

1940, August 11, College Theatre, Bennington, VT

El Penitente, Louis Horst
Letter to the World, Hunter Johnson

1941, August 10, College Theatre, Bennington, VT

Punch and the Judy, Robert McBride

1942, March 14, Chicago Civic Opera House, Chicago, IL

Land Be Bright, Arthur Krentz

1943, December 26, 46th Street Theatre, NYC

Salem Shore, Paul Nordoff
Deaths and Entrances, Hunter Johnson

1944, December 30, Library of Congress, Washington, DC

Imagined Wing, Darius Milhaud

Hérodiade, Paul Hindemith
Appalachian Spring, Aaron Copland

1946, January 23, Plymouth Theatre, NYC

Dark Meadow, Carlos Chavez

1946, May 10, McMillin Theatre, Columbia University, NYC

Cave of the Heart, Samuel Barber

1947, February 28, Ziegfeld Theatre, NYC

Errand into the Maze, Gian Carlo Menotti

1947, May 3, Cambridge High School, Cambridge, MA

Night Journey, William Schuman

1948, August 13, Palmer Auditorium, New London, CT

Diversion of Angels, Norman Dello Joio

1950, January 4, Columbia Auditorium, Louisville, KY

Judith, William Schuman

1950, January 22, 46th Street Theatre, NYC

Eye of Anguish, Vincent Persichetti
Gospel of Eve, Paul Nordoff

1951, December 5, Columbia Auditorium, Louisville, KY

The Triumph of St. Joan, Norman Dello Joio

1952, April 22, Juilliard School, NYC

Canticle for Innocent Comedians, Thomas Ribbink

1953, May 27, Alvin Theatre, NYC

Voyage, William Schuman

1954, March 18, Saville Theatre, London

Ardent Song, Alan Hovhaness

1955, May 8, ANTA Theatre, NYC

Seraphic Dialogue, Norman Dello Joio

1958, April 1, Adelphi Theatre, NYC

Clytemnestra, Halim El-Dabh

1958, April 3, Adelphi Theatre, NYC

Embattled Garden, Carlos Surinach

1959, May 14, City Center, NYC

Episodes: Part I, Anton Webern

1960, April 27, 54th Street Theatre, NYC

Acrobats of God, Carlos Surinach

1960, April 29, 54th Street Theatre, NYC

Alcestis, Vivian Fine

1961, April 16, 54th Street Theatre, NYC

Visionary Recital, Robert Starer

1961, April 20, 54th Street Theatre, NYC

One More Gaudy Night, Halim El-Dabh

1962, March 4, Broadway Theatre, NYC

Phaedra, Robert Starer

1962, March 5, Broadway Theatre, NYC

A Look at Lightning, Halim El-Dabh

1962, August 17, Palmer Auditorium, New London, CT

Secular Games, Robert Starer

1962, October 25, Habima Theatre, Tel Aviv, Israel

Legend of Judith, Mordecai Seter

1963, September 6, Prince of Wales Theatre, London

Circe, Alan Hovhaness

1965, November 2, 54th Street Theatre, NYC

The Witch of Endor, William Schuman

1965, November 3, 54th Street Theatre, NYC

Part Real–Part Dream, Mordecai Seter

1967, February 21, Mark Hellinger Theatre, NYC

Cortege of Eagles, Eugene Lester

1967, February 24, Mark Hellinger Theatre, NYC

Dancing Ground, Ned Rorem

1968, May 25, George Abbott Theatre, NYC

A Time of Snow, Norman Dello Joio

1968, May 29, George Abbott Theatre, NYC

The Plain of Prayer, Eugene Lester

1968, May 30, George Abbott Theatre, NYC

The Lady of the House of Sleep, Robert Starer

1969, April 11, City Center, NYC

The Archaic Hours, Eugene Lester

1973, May 2, Alvin Theatre, NYC

Mendicants of Evening, David Walker

1973, May 3, Alvin Theatre, NYC

Myth of a Voyage, Alan Hovhaness

1974, April 30, Mark Hellinger Theatre, NYC

Chronique, Carlos Surinach
Holy Jungle, Robert Starer

1974, July, Jerusalem, Israel

Jacob's Dream, retitled *Point of Crossing*, Mordecai Seter

1975, July 19, Uris Theatre

Lucifer, Halim El-Dabh

1975, December 8, Mark Hellinger Theatre, NYC

Adorations, classical guitar

1975, December 22, Mark Hellinger Theatre, NYC

The Scarlet Letter, Hunter Johnson

1977, May 17, Lunt-Fontanne Theatre, NYC

"O Thou Desire Who Are About to Sing," Meyer Kupferman

1977, May 24, Lunt-Fontanne Theatre, NYC

Shadows, Gian Carlo Menotti

1978, June 26, Metropolitan Opera House, NYC

The Owl and the Pussycat, Carlos Surinach

1978, June 27, Metropolitan Opera House, NYC

Ecuatorial, Edgard Varèse
Flute of Pan, Traditional

1979, December 9, Metropolitan Museum of Art, NYC

Frescoes, Samuel Barber, from *Antony and Cleopatra*

1980, April 29, Metropolitan Opera House, NYC

Judith, Edgard Varèse

1981, February 26, Kennedy Center, Washington, DC

"Acts of Light," Carl Nielsen

1982, June 9, City Center, NYC

Dances of the Golden Hall, Andrzej Panufnik

1982, June 23, City Center, NYC

Andromache's Lament, Samuel Barber

1983, July 1, Herod Atticus Theatre, Athens, Greece

Phaedra's Dream, George Crumb

1984, February 28, New York State Theatre, NYC

The Rite of Spring, Igor Stravinsky

1985, April 2, New York State Theatre, NYC

Song, traditional

1986, May 27, City Center Theatre, NYC

"*Temptations of the Moon*," Béla Bartók, *Dance Suite*

1986, June 4, City Center Theatre, NYC

"*Tangled Night*," Klaus Egge

1987, October 3, City Center Theatre, NYC

Persephone, Igor Stravinsky

1988, October 13, City Center Theatre, NYC

Night Chant, R. Carlos Nakai

1989, October 3, City Center Theatre, NYC

American Document (revised), John Corigliano

1990, October 3, City Center Theatre, NYC

Maple Leaf Rag, Scott Joplin

About the Author

Marian Horosko is the author of four books—two of them text-books—and is currently education editor at *Dance Magazine*. A former member of the New York City Ballet, Horosko also performed as soloist with the Metropolitan Opera Ballet; in films (*An American in Paris, Royal Wedding,* and others); on Broadway (first production of *Oklahoma* and other shows); and in concerts and on television. She produced the longest running radio show on the arts, collected films for the New York Public Library's Dance Collection's first archive, and developed dance-related programs for public television (now PBS), WCBS-TV, and cable stations. She has taught at the High School for the Performing Arts and at the Fordham University at Lincoln Center. She is listed in *Who's Who in American Women* as dancer/educator/author.